AT THE
STROKE
OF
ETERNITY

One Woman's Remarkable Near-Death Experience
and the Divine Messages Received

BY

AMBER CAVANAGH

I dedicate this book to my husband, Mike,
and to my children, Grace and Wyatt.
I love you to the moon and back.

Contents

Introduction

My Life Leading Up to This Moment

First Steps

*The first few steps into this life do not
determine the path you will walk.*

*Your feet are small and the obstacles you
face seem insurmountable.*

Growth is unavoidable even if we try to fight it.

As we trudge through this human life, at times feeling lost,

our soul knows we are capable of conquering each lesson.

Trust your feet as you learn to overcome each obstacle you face.

Know in your mind, body, heart, and soul, you are not alone.

You may call it destiny or fate, I call it limitless power.

We are strong.

We can walk through even the most difficult lessons.

We can live each life with understanding and grace.

Nothing is insurmountable, even when your feet feel too small.

THIS IS THE story of the day I had a massive stroke, went to the Other Side and came back. What follows is an attempt to recount my life leading up to that moment, what I learned along the way, and how I became the person I am today.

From my first conscious memory at three or four years old, I just knew I was different. I could see and hear things other people couldn't and never really understood why. For a long time I thought adults just ignored the people around them, but I later learned that they weren't ignoring anyone. What I was seeing and hearing wasn't human; they were spirits from the Other Side.

I saw these spirits constantly and could tell when they were around, but I never knew how to communicate or interact with them. Heck, I didn't know how to communicate with my parents or anyone else for that matter. So, I kept my thoughts and feelings to myself and tried to shut everything out.

Over time, this made me feel angry and alone. I felt

different from everyone in my family and school, which made forming and maintaining relationships really challenging. Even when I made connections, I was so worried that they'd think I was crazy that I'd self-sabotage the friendship to avoid being embarrassed. I spent a lot of time by myself, playing with dolls and farm animals, reading books, writing poetry, and journaling.

For years, I kept having experiences with spirit, but I never talked about it. I kept it all to myself until one day when I was seven years old.

I vividly remember waking up in a panic after I had a horrible nightmare. Deep down I could sense that it was more than just a bad dream, it was a premonition. I'd had dreams before that had come true, but they were usually about a plane crash or some sort of animal attack that happened in a far off place and didn't directly affect me. But this time I just knew that someone around me, someone that I knew, was going to get hurt and there was going to be a lot of blood.

My gut told me that this would probably happen when I got to school, and I begged and pleaded with my mom to let me stay home.

"Something bad is going to happen," I said. "Please don't make me go."

But she just shook her head and said, "no." At the time, our family was struggling financially and she couldn't afford to miss work. And before I knew it, I was at school walking to class.

At first, everything was normal and it seemed like just another ordinary day. In the afternoon, we had lunch indoors before heading outside to play. That's when I noticed a kid playing on the monkey bars. I couldn't stop looking at him.

I watched as he moved back and forth, his little hands gripping the bars and his legs swinging freely below him. And then, in the blink of an eye, he tumbled and fell to the ground, his face hitting the hard metal playground on the way down. His mouth exploded in blood and his arm broke upon impact—exactly as I had seen in my dream the night before.

I was shaking.

This is all my fault. I thought. *I dreamt it and now it happened in real life. What if I caused this to happen?*

For years, I held onto the fear that I caused terrible events like this to happen and constantly blamed myself.

As I got older, I tried to shut off all my spiritual gifts and get rid of anything that made me feel like I didn't belong. By the age of thirteen, I discovered that if I smoked pot or drank a lot, I could block out the spirits and any psychic abilities that I had. So I did those things, a lot. It was hard because I didn't feel like I belonged in my own body and I was willing to do anything to feel differently.

I remember staring at myself in the mirror and repeating my name over and over. *I am in this body, but I just don't recognize myself. This feels so weird.* As I was doing this, I was acutely aware that it wasn't dissociation. It felt more like a deep understanding in my soul that I was just uncomfortable with being in physical form. Even as a kid, I knew that I was more than just the person looking back at me in the mirror. I was a spiritual, energetic being having a human experience.

By the time I reached the age of fifteen, my family and I relocated to Mexico, where my dad opened a restaurant. It was during our time there that I experienced a really profound vision that changed my life.

The moment unfolded when I was walking alone one day, and suddenly, the sky lit up and it became really bright. In that instant, two paths opened up in front of me. Down the first path, I could see all of my friends and the drinking and partying, and all of the awful thoughts I had been having about myself. Down the second path, there was a beautiful, glimmering light. The intensity of it was overwhelming, but I wasn't scared.

That experience helped me begin to see that I had been running away from who I am my whole life. I could recognize all the ways I was working against myself and bringing myself down, and I didn't want to live like that anymore. I was ready to change my life. From that day on, I didn't touch another substance.

I stayed in Mexico for a couple months before returning to Canada. Living with my family was detrimental for me, so I asked my parents to give up rights over me so I could get assistance from the government for rent. They were struggling financially, so they agreed.

I then moved in with a friend's family and rented a room. I got back into school and started getting amazing grades. During this time, my mind often wandered back to the profound vision I had in Mexico. Initially, I equated it with a religious experience, so I began a journey of spiritual exploration.

I attended churches of many different faiths. I'd try one

out for a few weeks, then I'd try another one, and I kept going until I had visited ten or fifteen of them. Each church I went to was beautiful in its own way, but I didn't resonate with the judgment attached to their beliefs. I have never liked humans telling other humans how to live or what to do. The churches I visited just didn't feel like where I belonged. So, I kept looking.

Eventually, I found a church that felt like it suited me. It spoke to me because they weren't hyper focused on condemning anyone. And that's where I met my ex-husband, who was a prominent member of the church. We dated for awhile, and by the time I was seventeen years old, I found myself in a meeting with him and his parents. We explained that we wanted to move in together and asked for their blessing.

When his parents heard what our plans were, they responded, "No, you shouldn't do that. That's a sin. Why don't you just get married?" And in the course of an hour, it was decided that we were going to tie the knot. I felt I really didn't have much of a say, as I was desperate for help and a home. For the previous two years, I had bounced around from house to house, living with anyone who would take me in.

A month after I turned eighteen, we were wed. I picked a wedding dress off a sales rack at a local store, but the church planned everything else. The church leadership coordinated the ceremony and a potluck dinner—it was all very strict and highly regimented. Although they didn't allow dancing (that was considered a sin), my then-husband and I did share a first dance because it was a moment I had always dreamt of having. His parents turned their chairs away from us so they wouldn't have to watch something ungodly.

Looking back on it now, I'm not upset. Yes, the church was very strict and things were handled in an unconventional way. But I think the experience saved my life. When I was a teenager, I was headed down a very dangerous path. I had just left my parents, I was living on my own, and struggling to work and make money while keeping good grades in school. It was exhausting. In a way, finding that church helped me find myself.

I was married to that man for a few years until two of my close friends died in a tragic accident. When I heard the news, I was completely crushed and spent a week attending gatherings in their memory. At first, my husband was supportive, but his patience ran out fast. He truly believed in his heart that my friends would be damned to hell because of their religious beliefs (or lack thereof.) I can't fault him for that belief, because at that time in my life, I was walking those beliefs with him. But witnessing his lack of empathy became a deal breaker for me. I couldn't stand the thought of religion standing in the way of human decency and compassion for the loss of two teenagers, so I chose to leave the marriage.

At the time, it felt really empowering because it gave me a chance to get everything back that I felt I'd lost. I got my own apartment and filled it with furniture and things I loved, just to prove to myself that I could do it alone. I created a life for myself and it was going pretty well.

After about a year, I came to the realization that I had been working tirelessly to earn money to buy all these things, yet none of that stuff was really making me happy. Deep down, I knew something had to change. So, I decided to sell all my belongings and move to Asia.

I lived in Taipei, Taiwan, for two years where I spent my free time exploring the countryside and doing some serious soul searching. It was an absolutely amazing experience and I don't regret one minute of it. It was the first time in my life that I could just be me. Slowly, I started discovering who I was, what I liked, and finally let go of the need to apologize for merely existing. It was so freeing for my soul.

At the end of my second year there, I returned home to celebrate Christmas and that's when I met my husband, Mike. It was an instant connection, and I knew right away that I wanted to stay with him. Honestly, I didn't see it coming at all. In my mind, I'd planned on being in town for just a few days, but I ended up moving home for good. I had all of my things from Taiwan shipped back to Canada and we started dating pretty seriously.

During this time in my life, I began to notice how much I'd suppressed my authentic self, making compromises to fit into religious or societal molds or to please others. I was uncomfortable showing people the true me because in the late 90s, talking about seeing dead people or anything related to mysticism was considered pretty weird and sometimes frowned upon. Those days when most people thought about psychics, they'd picture the 1-900 numbers you'd have to call and pay $2.00 per minute to get all of your questions answered. That kind of thing just wasn't me. What I was experiencing with spirit was real and I finally felt open to talking about it, especially with Mike.

Fast forward a few years, and Mike and I got married when I was twenty-five. A year later, we had our daughter, Grace, and twenty-two months after that we had our son, Wyatt. It was such a wonderful time, but it went by way too fast. It felt like a blur. What I do remember is that I was finally smiling again.

I was unapologetic about who I was and felt more comfortable accepting my spiritual gifts. If you could have seen my Google searches you probably would have laughed—I was constantly diving into subjects about empaths, psychics, and mediumship. I loved it and wanted to learn more.

One thing I knew for sure is that I could hear spirit very clearly, but I'd never met anyone else who had that ability. I'd always assumed I was the only one who could hear it. Then one day that all changed.

It was very early in the morning on December 28th, 2015, before the sun came up. Mike was already awake, preparing for another day at work, while I remained curled up in our bed. He didn't turn any lights on because he wanted to let me keep sleeping.

As he was getting dressed, a sudden, unexpected sound of a child whining startled both of us.

Mike turned on his phone flashlight and yelled, "Wyatt! Go back to bed!"

I turned over and asked, "You heard that?"

"Yes!" Mike said. "One of the kids was in here messing around. You heard that too, right?"

"Oh, I heard it," I said. "But that wasn't one of the kids. That was a spirit."

Mike flipped the light switch on, and looked all around our room, even under the bed. Finding nothing, he went out into the hallway, looking for Grace and Wyatt. But when he checked on them, they were sleeping soundly in their beds. It was then, I believe, that realization began to click for him. Everything I'd been talking about with spirituality was real.

Later that same day, I decided to do my first practice psychic reading for someone. When I sat down to do the reading, a little girl spirit came through to me with a very clear message: she had passed away about a year before, and the anniversary of the day she first got sick was coming up soon. She asked me to contact her parents to let them know that she was okay, she knew they had been having a hard time since she died. When I gave the parents the message from their little girl, they were relieved and grateful, and it made the spirit happy too. After that, my connection to the Other Side just got stronger.

By February 2016, I started my business, West Coast Medium. I was doing a ton of psychic medium readings for friends and family and was doing free readings in mediumship practice groups on Facebook. This helped me build confidence and provided confirmation that the messages coming through were mostly accurate.

I was excited for this new path and wanted to share what I was doing with more people so I decided to tell the people at my church about my gifts. Their response wasn't great. The church leadership said the empath and mediumship stuff was okay, but any psychic gifts were not. In their perspective, possessing psychic talents equated to being a false prophet. But I just could not agree. Nothing I was doing felt wrong or against God. That's when I made the difficult decision to leave the church.

Very quickly after that, my business grew. And before I knew it, I had a full client list.

In the beginning, I really struggled with boundaries and made a lot of mistakes. I'd tell clients about health and medical issues, answer pregnancy questions, and get into a lot of stuff

I probably shouldn't have. It was a challenge for me because the more I did it, the more my spiritual gifts grew. I felt like the world became ten times louder because I was picking up on everyone's energy and everyone's thoughts. I had to learn an entirely new way of living and setting boundaries, and that took time. After a lot of trial and error, I started to feel balanced again.

Three years into my business, I was doing live mediumship events where more than two hundred people attended. I loved getting dressed up and doing readings for audiences like that. I also started hosting smaller groups, classes, and offering private readings in person and online. I had complete faith that I was exactly who I was supposed to be, doing exactly what I was supposed to do, without question.

I'm a medium, which means I can connect with people on the Other Side. I'm also an empath times a million, so spirit helps me see, feel, hear and sense things other people can't. I can feel every person on this planet because I can read their souls. I'm spiritually intuitive or what some may call psychic, which means spirit can provide guidance for the future or insight from the past if it is going to help or provide validation for you. I'm a medical intuitive, although I'm cautious with those gifts. I will tell people things if the issue is easily treatable, preventable, correctable, or fixable. If it's not, and it's something your soul has chosen to go through, there is no point in saying those things. I'm also a healer, but that gift is limited. If it's not meant to be healed, I can't take it away. I'm also an animal communicator, which I love.

My wish is as you read this story, my words may offer you hope and inspiration while answering some of your biggest questions about life, death, and the mysteries of the Other Side.

Chapter 1

The Day Time Stopped

The Light

In an instant a life can change.

It may come from discomfort or joy, sadness or pain.

We may not understand the purpose of each change as it comes.

One day you recognize yourself, you are confident in your purpose.

Then something shifts, your world becomes an unfamiliar shadow.

*You know somewhere deep inside, the person
you were is screaming to get out.*

The screams fall on deaf ears, as you struggle to stay afloat.

*Just as you are about to give in, and let the
comforting darkness envelope you.*

You catch a glimpse of your brightly shining soul.

In that moment a sliver of hope peeks through the shadows.

You recognize this place, you have been here before.

The strength to climb back into the light was always within you.

You just had to experience the darkness to celebrate the light.

DECEMBER 23RD, 2021, Nanaimo, Canada, 4:35 am. A sense of unease comes over me as I open my eyes. Here I am, lying in bed—but my body feels strange, and my mind is wrapped in a thick haze. I can't shake the feeling that something is very wrong.

What is this? What the hell is going on? Okay, I think to myself, *maybe I'm still dreaming. Bathroom, I decide. Maybe that will wake me up...*

Slowly, I drag my legs over the edge of the mattress, using my left hand to prop myself up. With a determined exhale, I plant both feet on the floor, attempting to stand. But I collapse under my own weight, and the entire right side of my body bumps and grinds against the wooden under-bed storage drawers as I fall to the ground like a bag of flour.

In an instant, I find myself on the carpeted floor, completely horrified and confused. I can barely move my body and I can't talk. I'm not sure what to do. Slumped here, I keep wondering if this is some weird sleep paralysis or dream. But I know it can't be. I know I'm awake.

I lie on the carpet for a while, staring into the darkness of the room. I'm all alone.

God, it's so hard to see. I wish I would have turned on the light earlier. If only I could make my way out of here to get Mike. He'd been in the living room and must have fallen asleep there.

I can see the doorway in front of me, only about six feet away. I muster all the willpower I have, attempting to drag myself forward, but my body refuses to move. It's as if my entire right side is frozen. I open my mouth to yell, but nothing comes out.

The realization that I can't make it to the door washes over me and panic sinks in. Even though it's probably only been a minute or two since I've fallen, it feels like an eternity. My heart races as I start thinking about how long I might be trapped here.

But giving up is not an option. I take a deep breath and swing my left arm into the air, hitting my fist against the wall as hard as I can.

BANG.

BANG.

BANG.

BANG.

Mike jolts up at the sound of the four loud bangs. He knows something is not right. Earlier, he'd been startled by the sound of my falling, but when he heard nothing else, he drifted back to sleep. Now, he hears me again. Still groggy, Mike makes his way to the bedroom and opens the door. He sees me sitting on the floor, my legs spread in front of me.

"What are you doing?" he asks.

In my mind, I can hear myself answering him and trying to explain what happened, but all that comes out of my mouth is "Michelle." Michelle is my sister and one of my closest soul bonds on the Other Side. We are so much more than family. We're best friends.

"Michelle. Mmm mmm mmm Michelle Michelle," I say.

Mike walks toward me and tries to pick me up, but stops. My body seems so much heavier, it is like trying to lift dead weight. His brow furrows as he gently releases me and makes his way over to turn on the lights. When he turns back to look at my face, he notices that my right eye and mouth are drooping. I am sitting strangely hunched over, leaning back on my left arm.

Mike's eyes lock onto me, and he says, "I think you're having a fucking stroke."

His hands are shaking as he races to dial 911. I can hear him getting frustrated with the operator. She keeps asking him questions and it's taking forever.

"Amber, try to lift your arms!" Mike yells. "Lift your arms! Try to smile!"

I can't do any of it on the right side.

Desperately I try to answer him, but nothing comes out except the words "Michelle" and "fuck," mixed with a jumble of weird gibberish and mumbling sounds.

"Mmm mmm mmm Michelle Michelle."

"Fuck. Fuck."

My mom (who lives in our basement suite) comes into the bedroom now. Because her room is below ours, she heard me banging on the wall and wants to know what happened. She sees me on the floor and begins asking questions, repeatedly trying to get a response from me. I can hear myself answering her in my head, but nothing comes out. I watch as Mike explains what's going on, my mom listening in disbelief.

There is no sign of any emergency vehicles yet. Mike

calls 911 a second time to confirm our address. I can tell he's starting to get angry.

I've been huddled on the chilly carpet for what feels like forever and I'm desperate for warm clothes. *If I can get someone's attention, maybe they will get something for me to wear.* I try pointing at my body, motioning that I need help getting dressed. My eyes look around the room, seeking someone who might sense my silent plea for help.

I watch in relief as my mom finally understands and reaches into my closet, pulling out a three-quarter length, fancy white sweater and pajama pants. *I'm going to look strange wearing this at the hospital,* I think to myself.

Not long after Mom dresses me, I hear the ambulance arrive and the paramedics lumber into the bedroom. They move leisurely, with no sense of urgency. I see their eyes scanning me up and down as they try to determine what to do next.

"Yeah, it's not a stroke," one says.

"Yes, it is!" Mike responds. "She has all the signs! Just look at her!"

"No. No, it's not a stroke," he replies.

Mike frantically explains that he is certified in level three first aid and knows the signs.

They look at him with skepticism, then look back at me. One of the paramedics bends down on one knee, stares me right in the eyes, and lets out a sigh.

"Yeah, I don't think this lines up with a stroke," he says.

Mike is dumbfounded. "I can't be more clear. She is having a stroke. Look at her face! Tell her to raise her arms. She can't do it. I tried to pick her up. She feels like dead weight."

"Well, we don't think it is a stroke," he responds. "But we can take her to the hospital."

Unhurried, they get me onto a stretcher and start putting things together, preparing one medical bag until they move to the next one. I'm absorbed in watching them. They're moving so slowly. Do the paramedics think I'm just making this up? I mean, I'm sure they get misdiagnosed calls all the time, but the way they are acting is so bizarre. I don't drink and I don't smoke. I don't do drugs. I don't do any of the stuff that can cause a stroke. And having them look at me as a drunk housewife… I'm just thinking, *You guys are so wrong.*

I'm in the ambulance now, but they don't turn the lights on. They don't call anyone, even though they are supposed to contact the hospital for suspected strokes. We ride along for a few minutes in silence until I decide to grab the arm of the paramedic who is sitting next to me and we make eye contact. I'm so scared. I can't talk. I'm just feeling panic. And at that moment, he truly sees me and finally realizes how droopy my face is.

"I think she's actually having a stroke," he says to the ambulance driver.

Unfortunately, they still don't do anything differently.

We arrive at the hospital, where they wheel me into the triage area. I can see gurneys everywhere and people coming in from other ambulances. The paramedics talk amongst themselves, completely ignoring me. Nurses and medical admission clerks stand in front of me, but face the opposite direction.

I wonder if they see me? No one is doing anything.
Why isn't anyone helping? What the hell is going on?

I want to scream, but no words come out, no matter how hard I try. A feeling of hopelessness overcomes me until I notice a nurse who, in his shuffle to find something, sees me out of the corner of his eye.

"What the hell are you guys doing?" the nurse yells. "She's clearly having a stroke, can't you tell?"

He picks up the phone beside him and calls a stroke code over the loudspeaker. Within seconds, medical staff are all around me, and everything's moving as if it's in fast forward. I can feel myself going in and out of consciousness.

Just as the chaos unfolds, Mike, who had called my sister Michelle earlier, and Michelle herself, arrive at the hospital. They are quickly approached by the primary triage nurse and doctors.

"We need to stop Amber's stroke by giving her a clot-busting drug called TPA (tissue plasminogen activator)," they explain.

My husband and sister both listen as the nurse goes through a general disclaimer about the medication and some of its risks. One of the dangers in stroke patients is that they will see a worsening of bleeding in the brain, which can be fatal.

"So, you understand," they say. "This could kill her, but it could also save her life. Do you want to do this?"

Without hesitation, Mike makes the decision. "Yes, just do it."

Usually, stroke patients see improvement immediately when given TPA, but this isn't the case for me. The doctor looks at us with solemn eyes and explains that my first stroke probably started at about 11:30 pm the night before.

"Too much time has gone by," the doctor explains. "The first stroke has already completed, which means the entire MCA 2 has been affected, but the TPA medication was able to stop the second stroke from progressing any further into the frontal lobe of her brain."

The brain tissue affected by the first stroke is already dead, the damage has been done and is not reversible. That's the funny thing about strokes. They don't hurt. They don't wake you up in your sleep. They just happen.

I hear the doctor explain to Mike that I will most likely be paralyzed on the right side of my body for the rest of my life. I can't feel anything when they do a poke test. There is not even a shadow of movement.

Michelle looks over at me and notices red, blotchy patches swelling all over my neck and chest. She senses my sudden discomfort, and I can hear the desperation in her voice as she calls for help.

Within seconds, I'm surrounded by nurses who swarm all

around me. I am going into anaphylactic shock, allergic to the Benadryl they gave me with the TPA therapy. One of them reaches over me and works quickly to stop the medication flowing through my IV. I feel helpless. There's nothing I can do but lie here and wait.

Once the Benadryl stops, I can feel my body stabilize, but the nurses are still in a panic.

"Okay. I know this is moving fast, but we must move Amber to another hospital," the nurse explains to Mike. "Because the TPA was unsuccessful, the only other option is brain surgery and we are not equipped to do that here. There's another hospital two hours away. We'll have to life flight her there. You're going to want to call your family so they have a chance to say goodbye before she goes."

I watch as Mike texts our kids. "Your Nanny and Papa are going to bring you to the hospital now." Next, he and Michelle start calling and texting all our close friends and family. Unfortunately, it is still very early in the morning so it was no easy task. But not even an hour passes before I see everyone rushing in to see me—my kids, my sisters, our parents, and extended family. Everyone is on pins and needles as the doctor comes out to talk with them.

"Her brain is dying," the doctor explains. "We need to send her to another hospital to see if there is anything they can do. She might not survive the trip."

I feel myself going in and out of consciousness again. Tears run down my face. I have never felt so scared. I can hear my family outside my hospital room talking amongst themselves. Some of them are in shock; they can't believe what's happening. Others are restless and angry. I can hear one of them confronting the hospital staff, "What do you mean that's all you can do for her? Let's get her to the other hospital!"

They take turns coming into my room now. As soon as a few people leave, more family members come in—it's like a revolving door. I know they are trying to say hopeful and encouraging words, but I can see the fear in their eyes. They don't think I'm going to make it.

As much as I love them, all I can think about is how much I want to see my kids. Since they arrived at the hospital, Mike hasn't let them get close to me. He's worried about how they'll react and doesn't want them to be traumatized.

I try to ask to see Grace and Wyatt over and over, but all that comes out is "Mmm mmm mmm, Michelle Michelle." No one understands me. They keep sending my sister Michelle into my room, but that's not who I want. I try making a cradle motion with my left arm to signify that I want to see my kids.

"Michelle Michelle."

They send Michelle back in again.

No! I think to myself. *That's not what I want! Can't they see I'm trying to ask for my kids?*

A nurse sees what's happening and quickly intervenes. I watch her as she approaches Mike.

"I know this is hard, but your children will resent you forever if they don't get to see their mom one last time to say goodbye."

With a deep breath, Mike looks down and nods. Finally, he lets the kids into the room with me. Relief washes over me as they approach my hospital bed. Grace, only fourteen, and Wyatt, just twelve, stand beside me as we hold each other and cry. It's the first time we've seen each other in what feels like hours.

"I know you're not going to die," Grace says reassuringly. "I know you're going to be fine. I love you." She's the strongest girl I know.

Wyatt struggles to speak. He's always been a quiet,

sensitive soul. We look into each other's eyes and he whispers through his tears, "I love you, Mom."

They are both devastated and so am I. Before they leave the room, they say "I love you" one last time. I wish I could say it back.

I hear an angry nurse on the phone with the helicopter pilot. He's supposed to fly me to the other hospital, but he doesn't want to come because of some expected bad weather. We will be getting a major snowstorm and he doesn't think it's safe.

The nurse pushes back. "You're going to get here. Right now," she demands. "I'm not going to have these children watch their mother die on Christmas because you can't get here. She will not survive a two-hour ambulance ride."

What she said must have convinced him because before too long, the hospital staff tells us that the helicopter has finally arrived.

My family is crying and afraid to watch me go. They all surround me, offering hugs and telling me how much they love me. I stare up at them with wide eyes as I get moved onto a stretcher and into the hallway.

"Okay, we need to go," Mike says as he hurries everyone along. "We need to save her life."

The hospital staff loads me onto the helicopter. They usually don't let anyone come with you, but they make an exception for Mike because they don't want me to die alone.

Me being rolled to the helicopter, barely clinging to life. Mike is walking behind.

What follows are true accounts from some of my loved ones who were there with me that day:

My sister, Michelle:

We say our goodbyes and watch the helicopter take off, then rush back to our cars to go home and pack. I sit down in my car, and for the first time I fall apart. I take a deep breath and allow myself to cry. A sound I have never heard before comes out of my body. A deep, guttural cry. I'm sure it is similar to the sound you would hear when a mother loses a child. I hope I never have to hear that sound again.

Driving home, I am reflecting on Amber and what she means to me. She is my closest person in this life. When I am stressed or anxious, I call her. When she is stressed and anxious, she calls me. We are able to talk each other off the highest ledge every time, and all I can think is I'm not ready for this. I want to call Amber because I'm scared and anxious and the thought crosses my mind that I might NEVER be able to call her again in these situations. The thought is unbearable.

I think about her kids. I am so scared for them. I want to do everything I can to keep them safe. To make sure they aren't scared. I love them like my own and I wonder how much of this they understand. Do they realize how serious it is? How will they cope if she doesn't make it? No, stop thinking like that. She's going to be okay. She has to be.

I start to think about how important Amber is for the world. Back when she first accepted her gifts, and I saw for myself what she was capable of, I had this thought that her life was just so important. Her life was more important than mine. We need her here, to bring us all a little piece of heaven.

Losing her would have such a huge impact on so many people and the idea of it happening felt so incredibly unfair.

My daughter, Grace:

After mom got on the helicopter, it was crazy. They were bringing her to the hospital in Victoria, which is two hours away, not counting rush hour traffic. It was so stressful because we were in a hurry, but Grandpa wanted to take a video of everything going on and it felt like we were moving really slowly. When we finally got back to our house, me and Wyatt shared a suitcase and packed another for Dad and Mom. We loaded these three large suitcases into the car and finally got back on the road. Somewhere along the way, Grandpa stopped at a Burger King and decided to get some food. I'm thinking to myself, what the hell? Our mom is dying, and we're stopping for a 2-for-1 meal. Me and Wyatt don't want to stop. We just wanted to get to the next hospital so we could see our mom.

Chapter 2

Beyond and Back

Home

I blinked and that was all it took.

The weight of being human, gone in an instant.

No more pain, no more suffering, it all made sense.

The continual question that creeps into
every corner of our lives, why?

There is no more why.

In an instant, I was able to embrace my past, present, and future.

It rolled away from me like waves, every thought,
concern, lesson, perfectly planned.

I opened my eyes, taking in the familiar energy that radiated
from the smallest blade of grass to the highest soul.

I was home.

THE SUN SHINES through the windows as the helicopter lifts into the air. It's been about seven hours since my stroke and I can feel my brain swelling inside my head. The pressure is unbearable. Everything inside me is heating up, and it feels like my body is on fire.

They must have given me a lot of drugs, I think to myself. But it isn't the drugs affecting me at all. My body is shutting down.

Up to this point, I was terrified of dying and was really scared by this whole experience. But something happens when you're close to death. That fear kind of morphs into something else. It just feels different. Peaceful almost.

Mike sits next to me. He pulls out his phone and explains that Wyatt texted him because he was afraid he didn't say enough when he was in the hospital room with me. As sunlight fills the helicopter, Mike reads me this message:

∽

I love you so much, I can't even say how much I love you,

and I will always love you no matter what. I have been rude to you these last few months, and I am so, so sorry. I would do anything to make me in the situation you are in and you to be back to normal. I will always be your baby boy, and will do everything I can to make you feel happy. After all of this we will go on a super long walk to Cottle Lake or maybe the foothills. I will walk until my feet fall off to make you happy.

Love you more than I can comprehend, Wyatt

I look up at Mike, then look away and close my eyes. The light coming through the windows is so bright. Mike lifts his arm to try to block the sun and at that moment *snap* I'm gone.

One minute I am in my body and fully aware of everything going on, and the next I'm completely detached from myself and everything else. I didn't have to go to the light; I didn't choose to leave. Nothing pulled me there, it just happened in an instant. Whether I'm alive or dead, I'm not sure. But in my soul, I know this is what people call the Other Side.

When I open my eyes, I find myself in the most beautiful garden I've ever seen in my entire life. There aren't words to describe how breathtaking everything is. I'm in a lush meadow, with vibrant green grass and delicate flowers blowing gently back and forth in the soft breeze. The colors here make Earth seem like a beige wasteland.

Each stone, tree, and flower contain its own unique energy, emanating with healing iridescent, golden light. I feel the life of the ground I step on, and I can connect with it. What seems at first glance like separate things are not separate at all. Everything and everyone is working together, harmoniously in sync. Just like each blade of grass is connected and inspired by the next, each soul is joined in mutual support, held together by unconditional love.

The innate oneness here is beyond description. Everything I can see beats with the same heart; the same energy flows through every fiber. Even the air is alive.

Some of my paintings post stroke, trying to
capture the energy of the garden.

I've always loved the color blue.

A white wooden gazebo is next to me, with a sparkling blue creek running underneath it from a pond on the other side of the field. I sit on a bench beside the gazebo and let the sunshine wash over me. It feels like coming home to the best place I've ever lived. I've never been more at peace.

I look down and notice I'm wearing a white off-the-shoulder eyelet dress and my body is that of my twenty-five-year-old self. My physical appearance looks the same, but the best version of myself. No wrinkles. No gray hair. All marks of time gone, every scar healed. The pain and discomfort in my physical body are no longer a part of me.

Somehow, I just know all the answers to any questions I've ever had about what has happened or will happen. I understand what my life would have looked like if I had chosen to take another path. I can see the ripple effects and outcomes of any scenario. Anything I've ever wanted to know is clear in my mind. There is no confusion. There is no panic. No fear. There is only clarity, peace, calm, and the most all-consuming, all-encompassing feeling of love.

Everything I'd ever struggled with, every doubt in faith becomes crystal clear. I see the past and everything that has ever happened in my life. All of my experiences. Everything that had hurt me. Everything that had brought me joy. It all made sense. And suddenly I realized there was no reason to ask why certain things happened. It was all just learning. I was learning. They were learning. We are all learning together.

On the outskirts of the garden, I see people looking lovingly toward me. I quickly realize that they are my husband Mike, my kids, my mother-in-law, my dog, and a few other people I know, both still alive and dead. I'm aware my husband and kids did not cross over with me, and that what I'm seeing are their higher selves or souls.

We look at each other from afar, but don't approach one another and don't speak. I know deep inside that I'm not here to interact with them. Instead they are here so I know I will be with them regardless of the decision I am about to make. Talking to them is not why I'm here in this place at this moment.

I look across the meadow and catch a glimpse of a different group of people standing near the back of the garden.

Who the heck are all these people? I wonder.

Each is from various times in history, some from the 1600s, 1700s, and 1800s, and some from the future. Others have origins in different dimensions and they are all different genders. I stare at them, trying to figure out why they're here, who they are, and then it dawns on me—each of these beings is one of my other lives. I can see a piece of my soul in each one of them and I am grateful they are here. You see, in this place, time and space don't exist. Everything and everyone lives simultaneously.

I find myself silently gazing at them when, unexpectedly, a sudden presence appears—my spirit guides have materialized, sitting beside me on the gazebo bench, one on each side.

"Your physical body is clinging to life, but barely," they explain. "You came here so you don't have to endure the pain and trauma. Now, you need to decide whether you want to stay here or go back to the life you were living."

I can hear everything they're saying, but they don't verbally say a word. All of our communication is telepathic. On the Other Side, you don't need to speak. You don't have to use language to communicate what you're feeling or what you want. The souls around you just know, they can feel it. And that's part of the beauty of being here.

On Earth, everything is so hidden. We don't show our true selves to each other. On the Other Side, there are no secrets.

There is no need for them. When you're in the afterlife, there is no judgment. There is no criticism. There is only love.

"If you go back, you need to understand what is going to happen," my guides explain. "The first eighteen months are going to be the hardest and worst eighteen months of your life. It's going to be extremely difficult to endure. It will challenge you in every way. You have not had an easy life, but this will be much more challenging than anything you have experienced. You are going to learn a lifetime's worth of patience in a very short period of time. You are going to wish you would have stayed here. But there are things your soul is still capable of. You will go from a life of learning to one of teaching, and the transition will almost break you. You are meant to write books, be a public speaker, and help the collective consciousness of the world move forward. You need to know the path to that life will be wrought with pain."

I can hardly believe what I'm hearing. Writing books? Public speaking? I've run away from becoming well known my entire life. Up until this point, I've been focused on raising my kids. I'm not super outgoing. I don't like strangers knowing my personal business, especially since I tried to hide who I was for so long. I've shared some on social media, but nothing major. I've always turned down every invitation to go on TV and really limited the number of podcasts or radio interviews I do.

Now my guides are telling me that returning to my life would mean I'd have to do all of those things. I'd have to let the world in. Not only would I be doing more social media appearances if I returned to my human body, but I'd be responsible for helping people figure out their life purpose and contributing to the collective enlightenment at a pivotal time in human history. It was a lot to take in.

"If you decide to go back to your human body, it is going to be equally hard and easy for you," My guides explain. "It will be a struggle because you are going to be human with human feelings and pain. But it will be more rewarding than anything you have experienced in this human life."

I look at them and nod.

"But you know," my guides continue, "if you choose to stay here, you will be ok too. You will just fully cross over and stay on the Other Side."

My guides take time to show me what this option would look like. They show me the fullness of the Other Side and how serene it would feel. They explain that I'd still be with my family and my kids in spirit, even if their physical bodies remain on Earth. They show me what my kids would do and what my husband would do if I died and how they would cope. I can see the trajectory of the rest of their lives and how it would change after they lost me.

As a human, things like this can be really hard to look at. But when you're on the Other Side, it doesn't feel that way. When you're a soul, you have a complete understanding of everything and everyone and never experience any stress or anxiety. As a soul, you don't experience any negative emotion at all.

Having this perspective helps me wrap my head around it. It helps me understand that if I choose to stay on the Other Side, my family would have to endure without me, learn to live without me, and heal after experiencing severe trauma. I would never want my family to suffer. I love them so much. But at this moment, the one thing I know for sure is that they would be okay no matter what I decide to do.

"If this is the end of this life for you, everything will be alright" my guides say. "The decision to stay or go is yours. There is no judgment. No punishment. There is no wrong choice."

As they communicate with me, my guides don't give me

their opinion. They never tell me what to do. I don't experience any pressure. It is an experience that makes me feel loved and supported. Together, we weigh the risks and benefits of each option in a very objective, matter-of-fact way, and they leave me alone to reflect on what I want to do.

This is when I take some time to experience everything around me. I squish my feet into the lush grass and revel in the energy which emanates from it. Barefoot, I make my way to the stream, wading into its gentle flow. It's like nothing I have ever felt before. The water shines with the light of God, each molecule carrying the presence of the Other Side.

Time becomes a distant notion as I get lost in this moment and ponder the choice I must make. As I do this, I am able to reflect on my life up until this point and I feel nothing but love and gratitude for my human self.

Existing even for this short amount of time on the Other Side allows me to access the collective consciousness and all of the knowledge we possess there. I do not have to ask what would happen, I just know. I am acutely aware of what the world struggles with and the potential impact of my existence is palpable. If I choose not to come back, it will be many years before someone like me will be born again. The circumstances in my life will be very difficult to recreate.

I feel a longing deep in my soul to return to my physical body. There is no longer a question of staying or going; I have to go back. My decision is made.

Suddenly my guides reappear and I am no longer alone in my thoughts. They tell me that since I've made up my mind, it is time for me to leave.

"What do you mean I have to go right away?" I ask. "I want to stay here and play in the grass and water!"

But they explain that staying any longer isn't an option, and within seconds I am removed from the garden and find myself in a waiting room filled with bright white light.

I see my body and my loved ones below, almost as if I'm looking at a movie screen. I see them plead and bargain with God, begging for me to live. I see my husband panicking in the helicopter, still trying to block the sun from my eyes.

"Please, I'll do anything," Mike says. "Just don't let her die."

Unlike when I was in the garden, there is nothing to distract me here. All I can do is observe what is going on around my physical body. I don't feel panicked or concerned about what is happening. Thankfully, I still have access to the peace, love, and serenity of the Other Side, so I just calmly watch as things unfold.

The helicopter lands in Victoria, the hospital staff ready and waiting for my arrival. The vibe is much different there. The staff seems calm and collected, completely prepared for what was to come. They wheel my body off the helicopter and back to the ICU, where the whole team waits to treat me. From above still, I watch as they move me down the hospital hallway, where they transfer me to a bed. Mike is still with me, and he looks so worried.

Within minutes, my entire body goes rigid and starts seizing. The nurse frantically starts yelling for help, causing Mike to panic and run out into the hallway, calling out for a doctor.

"Help! Somebody help!" They both scream now, desperate for someone to come.

With a seizure, there's not much you can do but protect the person from hurting themselves while you wait for it to stop. And that's exactly what the doctors do. I watch from the Other Side as my body shakes and seizes. They're monitoring my stats and trying to keep me safe. This goes on for about a minute until my body stops moving and goes completely comatose.

My spirit guides explain that if I had chosen to stay with them in the afterlife, this is what would have caused my death. The seizure would make my brain continue to swell to the point of no return, ultimately leaving me brain dead. However, I made the decision to come back, and that choice changed everything.

It's at this very moment that the Other Side fades away, and just as quickly as I had traveled there, I am back in my body, unconscious.

Chapter 3

Struggling

Renew

The lessons I am learning feel painful and hard.

Some days I wake up with my heart in shards.

I look all around me and I'm surrounded in love.

But I still search for the home I went to up above.

The decision was easy, to go back or to stay?

I knew it would be hard to return to life this way.

I was aware what was coming but it was easier there.

Life on this earth does not feel fair.

As I move through these lessons, I recognize the path.

They prepared me for hardships, that will not last.

So as I travel this road I look to above.

Because they will help me recover what was lost, my self love.

I LATER LEARNED that as I was laying there, unconscious in the hospital bed, an unexpected conversation took place between the neurologist and Mike.

The neurologist leans in with a serious tone and asks Mike, "Can I talk to you?"

He draws an image on his notepad. "See this? This is what's going on with Amber's brain."

The neurologist references my MCA2 artery. "Her stroke has already completed, which means all brain tissue fed by this artery is dead. At this stage, I don't know if there is much more we can do for her."

The severity of the situation sinks in as Mike listens, trying as hard as he can to understand everything that is happening.

"In this case, the only other option would be brain surgery where we would feed a tube through her groin into her brain to try to remove some of the clots," the neurologist explains. "It may not do anything, and there is a high probability it may cause another stroke on the other side of her brain. The TPA she was given at the first hospital makes her prone to bleeding. But we want to give you the option. Do you want to do it?"

"I don't know what to do," Mike says nervously. "If it were your wife, what would you do?"

"The risk of re-stroking and bleeding is so high," the doctor responds. "Right now, we don't know if she will live or die, and if she recovers, you may have to take care of her for the rest of her life. But there is a chance the surgery might kill her. If it were my wife, I wouldn't do it."

With a mix of fear and hope in his heart, Mike chooses to place his trust in the neurologist's expertise and declines the surgery.

When morning comes, I open my eyes and find myself all alone in my hospital room. At this point, I know I'm still alive, but it feels like a strange, foggy reality. I can remember the Other Side, but I am also painfully aware that my body is not doing so great.

I sit by myself in silence until I hear movement in the hallway. Then, the door to my room gently opens, revealing a few of my loved ones. It's hard because I want to talk with them, but I still can't communicate. So, I just watch and listen.

The neurologist approaches us slowly. His voice is low and

measured as he explains to my family that I've lost vision in my right eye, became paralyzed on the right side of my body, and will never be able to eat on my own again.

"She'll likely need a feeding tube and long-term care for the rest of her life," he says.

I can see it on everyone's faces, especially Mike's— a mix of shock and uncertainty as they absorb what they're hearing. It's clear that Mike is wrestling with the question: Did he make the right call when he told the doctor not to do the surgery?

It wasn't until later that we discovered if Mike had said yes to the surgery, I would have most likely died. The damage in my brain was too severe to fix, and I would have bled out uncontrollably. He didn't make my medical condition worse. Mike saved my life.

The room slowly fills with a steady stream of family members eager to hear how I'm doing. My eyes scan the constant shuffle of people, and then, like a light in the midst of the crowd, I spot them. My kids are here! I am so relieved to see them. I cry as they walk through the doorway and start making their way to my bed.

I close my eyes as we sit and hold each other. My heart is so overwhelmed with love, I just want to be with them forever.

Then, all of a sudden, another family member comes in and tells them they have to leave. As soon as I hear this, I start crying uncontrollably. I grab Grace's hand and hold it tight. I don't want to let go.

"What do you mean we have to leave?" Grace asks. "We've only been with her for a little while."

My heart is breaking. My kids are walking toward the door and I can't stop it. I stretch out my arm and reach for them. *Please don't make them leave. Please.* I plead in my mind. No one understands me. I'm forced to watch helplessly as my children are pushed away.

Grace stomps down the hallway and sits on the floor. She's in complete shock that the other adults would make her and her brother leave before they were ready. Grace sits in this spot for a while, blasting music into her AirPods as she tries to calm down.

Family members flow in and out of my hospital room until a few of them begin chatting about heading home. It's Christmas Eve and they want to get ready to celebrate the holiday. Amidst the shuffle, Grace and Wyatt come back into my room and I couldn't be happier to see them.

Unfortunately, visiting hours are very strict in the neuro

ICU as a lot of rest is needed for recovery. As night approaches, we find ourselves in a bittersweet goodbye, and Mike and the kids head to their hotel room where they watch the movie *Elf* and eat Indian food for dinner.

The next morning, Mike and the kids return to the hospital, excited to celebrate Christmas with me. The vibe in the room is so much lighter, and everyone seems so much happier. And during rounds, my neurologist comes up with an idea.

"How about you try singing Christmas carols together?"

He explains my speech center is damaged, but the part of my brain that controls singing and swearing is still functioning on the other side. So Mike and the kids start singing and miraculously I am able to join in! The whole experience feels magical, and I am glad they're recording it on their phones. These videos are the best Christmas gift my family has ever received. Mike later explained that it was during this moment that he really started to have hope.

My condition stabilizes little by little, and within the next two days I show massive improvement. I wiggle my toes first, then lift my arm. I talk slowly and with much difficulty. Although most words come out with some sort of "Michelle" attached to them, it is really amazing. I can finally form sentences! By day three, I'm walking down the hallway with the help of a nurse.

My neurologist, who has been in practice for more than thirty years, watches in astonishment.

"I've never seen anything like this. We don't understand," he says. "She is a miracle because there is no other explanation."

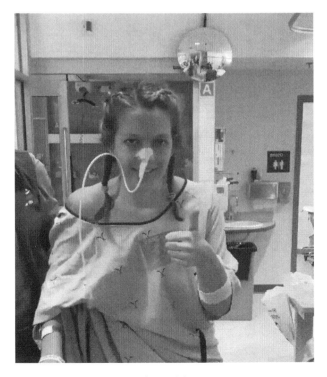

December 26th, 2021

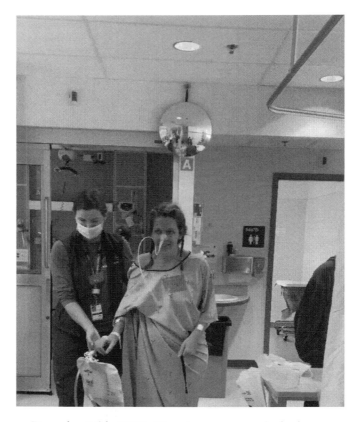

December 26th, 2021. First time up to use the bathroom.

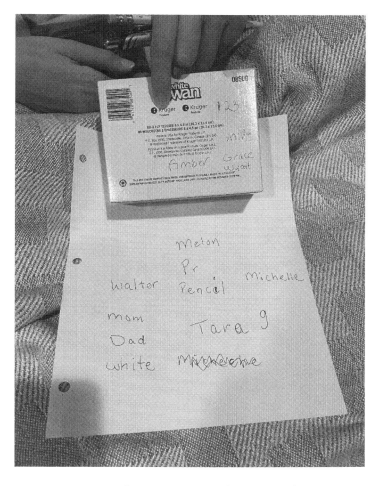

First words written since stroke on December 28th. Notice I scratched out Michelle because I was tired of saying it every second word.

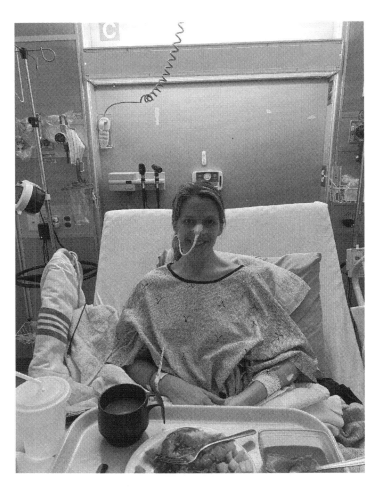

December 29th before they took away solid
food due to constant choking.

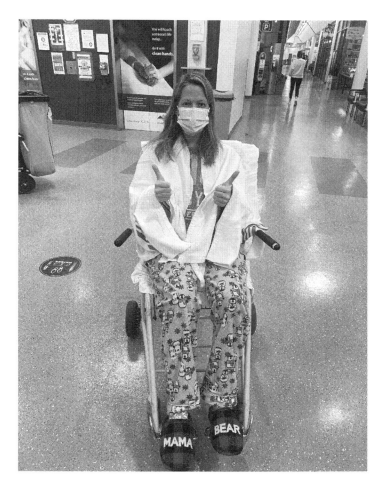

Leaving the hospital January 6ᵗʰ, 2022.

The kids seem relieved and almost amused by how different I am. Grace later recalled, "She's usually a very strict mother in the most loving way possible, but during the days after Christmas she is acting almost like a teenager. She is making jokes and saying inappropriate stuff, which we think is hilarious." Turns out that becoming somewhat childlike is a symptom of a massive stroke.

The neurologist is being really thoughtful and kind too. He's drawing pictures and breaking down really complex medical terminology so it's easier to understand. He's offering Mike and the kids advice about how to support me too.

"To help your mom heal, don't finish her sentences for her," he explains. "Let her figure it out. You can help her a little bit, but once she gets it, make her repeat it seven or eight times. This will help her brain create new pathways and help her remember those words for the future."

So they do. As much as it frustrates me, they let me figure things out on my own without telling me the answers or fixing things for me. I'm learning how to talk again.

For a while, things go really well until tragedy hits home again. Mike comes into my hospital room with tears in his eyes.

"We had to put one of the dogs down," he utters.

We are all extremely close to our dogs and consider them to be like family, which is why my response really surprises Mike.

I smile and wave my hand, "Oh, it's fine. It's fine," I say.

What I share with him is the truth. Deep down I know that everything is going to be okay because I saw my dog and all of my family on the Other Side. No matter what anyone says, no matter what happens, I know there is no need to worry.

After my NDE experience, nothing bothers me. The next few days I feel like I'm on a high. Everything feels so serene and positive, almost like I'm living in a beautiful dream.

And then out of nowhere, reality hits. Hard.

The all-encompassing peace and calm from the Other Side disappears, and the realization that I am a very brain-injured person with a long road ahead of me starts to sink in. I'm firmly rooted back in my body and it's horrific.

What the actual fuck? I think to myself. *My guides told me all these wonderful things, but I'm paralyzed on the right side. I'm eating out of a tube. I don't have any hunger or bathroom cues. I can barely walk. I can barely talk. I can't embrace my family. I'm stuck here like a prisoner.*

Days later, I wake up and notice a painful red rash. The

nurses say that because the rash started on the paralyzed side of my body that I didn't feel it progressing. It has gotten so bad now that it has spread and the skin all over my torso is covered in pin-prick blisters. It's excruciating.

They tell me it's an allergic reaction to one of the medications they are giving me, so they stop administering it and give me a cream that helps relieve the inflammation. But I'm still struggling so much.

My brain is horrifically swollen because of the stroke and I'm having some of the worst migraines of my life. The pain is taking over every cell of my body. There isn't one minute that passes where I'm not hurting and I can't stop thinking about how awful everything is. I've been in the hospital for over a week and I can hardly stand it anymore.

I can't help but wonder. *Why did I do this to my family? Why didn't I just stay on the Other Side?*

To make things worse, I find out Covid is breaking out on the hospital floor I'm on. The hospital is at only about 50% of their normal staff levels and they have completely full beds. Both the patients and the staff are getting sick and everyone is having a really tough time. I've been told I could get discharged to go home if I get a certain heart test, but I can't get an appointment to do it.

For my age, a common cause of stroke is being born with a tiny little hole in your heart called a PFO (patent foramen ovale.) Most people don't even know they have it, but once in a while, it can throw a clot. The doctors need to check for it just to be sure. The trouble is, to get my heart test, I need to have it done at another hospital that is capable of doing something so specialized. But because of Covid, I can't get in right away. So I'm stuck here, waiting.

Mike is still driving back and forth between the hospital and his hotel every day. He tries to be with me as much as he can, but he can't be here 24/7, so he asks the hospital staff to notify him anytime there's a change in my condition. They nod and agree, but the doctors and nurses keep forgetting. Instead of calling Mike, they're giving me a bunch of information which is really hard for me to understand and I usually end up forgetting most of it. My brain just can't retain it. After three or four missed visits, Mike loses it.

"She has a brain injury," he tells them. "You can't relay all of this important information to Amber. She won't be able to retain it. It's ridiculous to put that amount of responsibility on her. She almost died. You need to notify me immediately with information about her condition, improvements, or deficits."

Throughout all of this, the hospital staff keeps moving me. I start in the ICU, then go to the Neuro ICU. Next, I am moved to a double bed hospital room with an elderly woman who also had a stroke. This elderly woman lays in the bed next to me, completely unconscious and unable to move or talk. The only thing that people think will make her happy is hearing the song "Do-Re-Mi" from the movie *The Sound of Music*. The staff has it playing twelve hours a day on repeat. It's so awful, I can't stand it. The song just keeps playing over and over. It's crazy making. With a brain injury like mine, I just need quiet.

Eventually, Mike convinces the nurses to cut back on the music. They agree to play the song only when the elderly woman's sister is visiting and keep it quiet the rest of the time. I feel so much relief, but it doesn't last long. They're moving me again, this time into the hallway.

The next few nights, I lie on a stretcher right outside the nurses' station. Even though I feel like I'm in a really obvious place, it seems like no one sees me. The nurses talk constantly and go about their shifts without really acknowledging me. They don't even turn the lights down. All of this just compounds the pain. My brain hurts so badly that I pray for another stroke to kill me.

In the next four days, I get about five hours of sleep. I can't begin to describe how exhausted I am. A wave of despair overwhelms me, and I find myself sobbing uncontrollably.

Six long hours pass by as I lay here alone. No one notices anything until a nurse comes in the next morning for her day shift. When she sees me, she is so horrified and shocked that she runs to the phone to get help. She knows I'm waiting for a heart test and wants to find a hospital that can get me in.

"She's been here for days," the nurse says. "It's the last test she needs before she can go home. Just get her in!"

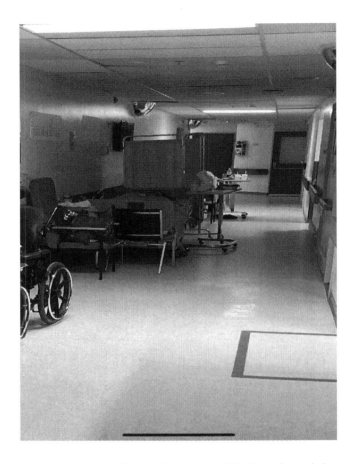

My bed in the hallway where I stayed for four days while waiting for a heart bubble test to check for a PFO (patent foramen ovale). If you look closely you can see me.

The nurse confirms with the other hospital that they can do the test that day. Now her task is to find me an ambulance so I can get over there, but it is taking forever. We had a huge dump of snow on the island, which is like Armageddon because nobody here has the capacity to deal with it. So I call Mike and ask, "If they can set it up, are you okay with driving me so I don't have to wait for an ambulance?" Mike agrees and races to pick me up.

He takes me to a hospital ten minutes away, and the car ride is horrible. The snow is so bright and the sound is too intense. It makes my eyes water and my ears ache, but I don't say anything. I can hardly wait to get this over with.

We arrive, and I finally am able to get the echocardiogram with a bubble test (plus a million blood tests and other heart tests.) There are no red flags. The doctors say I just won the wrong kind of lottery. No known cause for the stroke was ever discovered.

Once the tests are finally done, we are relieved to hear the best news ever—we are going home! Mike takes a picture of me smiling as I get discharged from the hospital. We eagerly make our way to the car. But what should have been a straightforward journey turns into the worst hour and a half of my life. My brain struggles to process everything, and I spend most of the drive covering my eyes, trying to breathe through the nausea and anxiety.

Finally, we arrive at our house and take the first steps through the front door. Christmas decorations are up and colorful presents are under the tree. My family's eyes are filled with warmth and anticipation, eager to celebrate the holiday with me. But I just can't do it. Every light and every sound feels like absolute torture.

For the past two weeks, I've been in the Neuro ICU hospital ward with nothing but very low stimulation. The lights are dim there. People talk quietly. There aren't as many beeps or sounds because brain-injured people have a really hard time with things like that. Walking into our home like this is just too much.

I'm still struggling with speech, but try to tell Mike how I'm feeling. "Everything is too loud. We have to do Christmas tomorrow." In the beginning, I describe anything unbearable as being "too loud."

After trying to explain, I walk into my bedroom to lay down, but I don't really sleep. Instead, I just lie in bed with the lights off while I stare into the dark, wondering what my life will become.

First morning home, January 7ᵗʰ. Also our Christmas morning.

Make-shift Christmas after I got home

Chapter 4

Recovery

Fog

She searches, and even as she catches a glimpse of what her
life could be, the walls continue to close in around her.

She knows this fog, although suffocating, can bring comfort.

She closes her eyes and pictures her life.

She acknowledges there will come a day where
the fog lifts and light can shine again.

She says this to herself, a mantra to help her walk
through this time where the darkness feels blinding.

Every great lesson of being human contains
light and dark, good and bad.

Fog rolls in, and lets us ponder the lessons we are learning.

Only when you recognize the deep knowledge you are
gaining as you walk through suffering, will your soul open
up to the possibility that for every dark moment, there is
an equal and infinite light just waiting to be let in.

She has gratitude for the darkness, and allows the light in.

THE HOSPITAL STAFF who treated me were scared out of their minds about what they saw happen. They'd rarely seen someone like me, a healthy forty-year-old woman with kids, have two massive strokes and a seizure and survive. In their experience, most stroke patients are in their seventies or eighties with major health complications. To see what happened to me was traumatizing, and many of them took it home with them. Most of them assumed I died or ended up being a vegetable, but weren't really sure. They would often talk amongst themselves about their memories of that experience, asking each other if anyone knew how I was doing.

One of my sisters, who has worked at the Nanaimo hospital for over twenty years, hears about how worried everyone is. She decides to share my story on the nurses' group Facebook page, reassuring everyone that I was not only alive, but doing well. Everyone is astonished and relieved.

By the time I go in for my first follow-up appointment, I am fully coherent, talking, and feeling fairly good. The neurologist is so impressed by my progress that he brings in some of the stroke nurses working that day just to see me.

"Can I take you in the hall to see if you can walk well?" he asks.

As I go up and down the corridor, they all watch in amazement and can't believe their eyes. Here I am, walking by myself with no wheelchair or support. Though I still use walking sticks in my day-to-day life, at this moment, the sight of my progress leaves them speechless.

Next, the neurologist invites me, Mike, and my sister to join him in the exam room where he shows us the first scans of my brain. Usually when people have a stroke, it shows up as a teeny tiny white dot on the MRI. My primary stroke is the size of a fist. My second stroke appears a little smaller, but is still large.

"This part of your brain is gone and will not regrow or heal," the doctor explained.

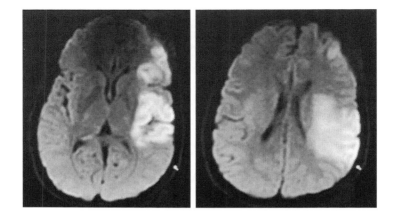

The MRI scans taken shortly after the stroke.

I have a really hard time accepting what he is telling me. When faced with an injury, my mentality has always been that you work hard, heal yourself, and get better. Unfortunately, with the brain, it just doesn't work like that. There is no reversing the problem. All the tissue damaged by the stroke just sluffs off and fills with cerebral fluid.

"It doesn't ever come back," the neurologist continued. "Your brain will simply remap as best it can. You may never get back to who you once were."

As I listen, the cold reality of my situation sinks in. Things aren't going to go back to normal for me overnight. This is going to take time and patience.

Thankfully, the hospital's rehabilitation center is allowing me to be an outpatient because we live nearby. I am deeply grateful not to be confined to a hospital room again, but they are requiring me to come back four days a week.

Throughout my entire recovery process, I work my ass off for every physical gain. It feels like an uphill battle every day. Countless times, I find myself so overwhelmed with frustration that I break down in tears.

The stroke caused retrograde amnesia, which means I can't remember the previous two years and the two years before that are extremely patchy. I also struggle with emotional lability constantly. I laugh when I want to cry and cry when I think I am laughing. I struggle to maintain normal emotions and feel like I'm behaving like a child in many ways. This whole thing is creating a huge learning curve for everyone, especially Mike and the kids. We have always been a light-hearted, joking family. But after the stroke, I can't tell if they are joking or serious. It is overwhelming for all of us.

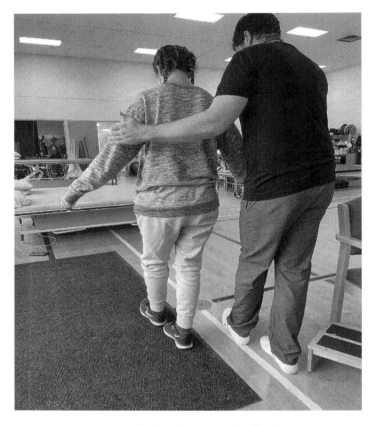

January 13ᵗʰ, first day in rehab after being
discharged from the hospital.

Communication is really tough too. When I had the stroke, I had so much damage on the left side of my brain that my entire language center was wiped out. Unbeknownst to me, because I'm left-handed, I must have been born with a second language center on the right side of my brain, which makes remapping my speech much easier. Thank God for being left-handed. If I wasn't, I may never have been able to talk again. I still struggle with words and can't understand or retain anything I read though.

When I do try to talk, it comes out like a cross between a baby and someone just learning English. It's tough because I can't quite figure out when to use inflection or change my tone, so I end up sounding kind of robotic. And when I want to express my needs or wants, it usually comes out as just a word or two because I can't put together more complex sentences.

To help me recover language, they have me using apps on an iPad in partnership with rehab. And honestly, it's so frustrating. I can't spell the most simple of words. The app will show me a picture of a kitchen and ask me to spell the word "kitchen" but I can't do it. When I look at the picture I can see the images, but I don't remember the word for the room I'm looking at. I can't figure it out. And when they ask me to unscramble the letters or put them together in a different order, I find it impossible. It's an ongoing struggle.

What makes it even more challenging is that every time I feel like I'm making progress with my recovery, there seems to be a major setback. Throughout the next five months, I am back in the hospital three times because I keep having transient ischemic attacks (TIAs), which are like mini strokes that cause a temporary blockage of blood to small areas of the brain. Evidently, these are pretty common in stroke survivors as they recover, but they can be really serious if they're not treated.

In March, my daughter decides to go out to a movie with her friends for the first time since the pandemic began. Unfortunately, a few days later, we find out that she's developed Covid, and it ends up spreading throughout our entire family.

The virus hits me hard and my body really struggles with it. I get so dehydrated that I wind up back in the hospital again. It's frustrating because my recovery is taking much longer than everyone else's.

Then, three weeks later, I wake up one morning with severe chest pain, and it is an immediate rush to the emergency room. The x-ray shows that I've developed Covid pneumonia.

Adding to the emotional turmoil, we had to say goodbye to my soul dog due to cancer just a few days before. The weight of it all is devastating.

My soul dog Walter

Over time, I start to heal and begin feeling more like myself. However, the doctors are concerned that all the stress on my body is putting me at risk of having another major seizure. As a precaution, they prescribe me a powerful anti-seizure medication unlike anything I've ever taken before. It makes my brain feel like it's on fire.

I explain it to Mike like this, "Have you ever spent a long night drinking, only to wake up the next morning so hungover that you feel like you're going to barf? Your body feels horrible, and you have a really bad headache? So, to feel better, you try drinking three cups of coffee, but that only makes your body feel like it's vibrating while you're slowly dying on the inside? Yeah, that's what this medication makes me feel like."

To make it worse, it also makes me think about killing myself, which I later discovered is a common side-effect for some people. I tell my neurologist what I'm going through and mention how worried I am that I'm experiencing suicidal thoughts.

"We'll have to work on switching your meds," he says. "But we'll have to do it very carefully. This isn't a medication you want to stop taking cold turkey."

So, my doctor creates a plan to wean me off the first medication while simultaneously introducing my body to a new, different anti-seizure medication. And for a time, I am taking them both at once. The combination makes me so sick that they admit me back into the hospital again because I can't stop throwing up.

My brain hurts so badly, it feels like knives are being thrown through my head. The pain is excruciating. And things just keep getting worse. My body is starting to give out, my white blood cells are in hyperdrive, and my hemoglobin is extremely low. Nothing is working the way it should.

Usually, people who have strokes start to see their brain

swelling go down after about six weeks. The swelling in my brain is taking much longer to dissipate. Every time the doctors take an MRI or CT of my brain, they seem confused. They just don't understand why it's still so inflamed. I know it's because of all the health challenges I keep getting hit with. It's been non-stop complication after complication.

Looking back on these first few months since the stroke, I can honestly say I would have rather been dead. I wouldn't wish this kind of pain on my worst enemy.

When I was on the Other Side, and I made the decision to come back into this body, it just looked so much easier. I had a totally different perspective as a soul looking down on the world. It was almost like looking down at a video game or hologram and thinking, *Oh yeah, life is going to be hard. But it's all temporary human stuff. I'll be fine.* But living through this experience and being in this physical body is a completely different thing.

Don't get me wrong. My spirit guides did warn me. They said I would wish I didn't come back to this physical reality. But they also reassured me that after the first eighteen months following the stroke, life would get better. That the experiences awaiting me would make it all worthwhile.

Deep down, I have faith that everything my guides said on the Other Side is true and there is a reason for all of this. But it is so hard to see through the drug haze and the brain damage to be able to fully grasp it.

I start to question myself and my purpose on this Earth. I mean, I'm one of the strongest psychics in the world, and I didn't even see this coming. Like, what the hell? It would have been nice if I had gone to the hospital that night with a severe headache, so they could have caught the stroke early on and prevented any severe damage. But oh, no. I had no warning. I had to go all the way and have two massive strokes that destroyed over two-thirds of the left side of my brain. I'm just like, *thanks so much, higher self, you did a bang-up job with this plan.*

Because of everything that's happened, I'm left with deficits I'll live with for the rest of my life. And today, I think, at least for people who watch me on social media or see me occasionally in person, I look pretty normal. I appear as an average, neurotypical person. But I struggle every day. Speech is still hard for me. I do pretty well with it in the morning, but come afternoon, I struggle to find words, and by nighttime, it's like a bad game of charades. This goes for texting, too. I have mostly given up trying to text in the evening as it's too difficult and takes me multiple tries to get it right.

I've also learned that the part of my brain responsible for organization is severely damaged by the stroke, so anything involving planning or sequencing feels almost impossible. I have trouble following the order of things. It's very hard for me to understand directions that come with things like cooking recipes because I can never remember what step comes next. I've found ways to work around it by writing things down, but it's still hard for me to stay on track.

And then, there's the right side of my body. It has no sensory feeling anymore, so I can't feel hot, cold, or pain most of the time. Trying to get the muscles and tendons there to cooperate is a daily struggle, and due to this, they have loosened up so much that my joints don't stay easily in place. This causes constant ongoing nerve and joint pain. As hard as it is, I refuse to take strong pain meds and can no longer take anti-inflammatories, so acetaminophen has become my best friend.

I also have a sound processing disorder. Although my hearing is fine, my brain can't make sense of what I hear the way it used to. So, if I'm ever talking too much, overwhelmed, or tired, I immediately feel like I need to pop my ears. It's echoey, almost like I'm underwater.

Having conversations with people is different now too. I used to be super witty around people, and now, especially if I'm in a crowd or large group, I am almost mute. It's like the sound processing disorder takes over and I can't focus and I can't understand. Often the conversation has moved on before I've wrapped my head around what's going on.

I've tried talking to doctors a few times about my symptoms, but they all say the same thing. "You shouldn't be alive. You should just be grateful that you've made as much progress as you have because we've never seen someone like you." So, I have no choice but to learn to live with it.

One of the other main issues is that the sphincters in my throat no longer work properly. Normally, the sphincters control flow from the throat to the stomach, as well as block food from entering a person's lungs. But when I eat, the food doesn't stay down; instead, it lingers halfway up the tube. Because that part of my body is somewhat numb, I don't experience heartburn. It just hurts, a lot.

I also experience ongoing issues with my mouth because I've lost sensory feeling. Usually, when an average neurotypical person eats, your brain will automatically tell your tongue to take any food you put into your mouth and form it into the shape of a ball. If it's a mixed texture like a soup, you will always swallow the liquid before you make a little ball with the solid food. The body does this because it makes it easier to swallow and prevents choking. Since my stroke though, my mouth can't separate the food from the liquid. I can't make the little ball out of the solid food, so everything forces its way through and goes down my throat all at the same time, causing me to choke all the freaking time. It's painful and it's happening to me all day.

Throughout it all, I try to have patience with everything that's happened and trust that there is a purpose behind it all, but it's still mind-boggling to me. My guides said I would accomplish all these things, but how will that be possible? Sometimes doubt creeps in and I think that maybe it's all bullshit. Maybe I made it all up. Maybe I will deal with this for the rest of my life.

But I know what I experienced on the Other Side was real. I chose to come back to this life and I made that choice full of love and positive intention. I'm here because I want to be and I'm going to make the most of it, even when life isn't easy. And I know in my soul I am supported not just in the spiritual realm, but by my family and friends too.

My mom Sue and me, Mother's Day 2023.

Lunch celebration with Mike, the kids, and me
December 23rd, 2022 for my Strokeaversary.

My best friend Megan and me before the stroke.

My beautiful family one year after the stroke.

*Left to right: My dad Fred, my son Wyatt, my
husband Mike, my brother-in-law Jeff.
April 19th, 2023.*

*From left to right: My sister Michelle, me, my daughter
Grace, and my mom Sue. April 19th, 2023.*

Christmas Eve 2022, one year after the stroke.
From left to right: Me, my sister Cheri, my mom Sue, my
sister Michelle, my dad Fred, and my brother Chris.

I asked a few of my family members if they wanted to share what this experience has been like for them. What comes next is from my sister, Michelle, my husband, Mike, and my kids, Grace and Wyatt, in their words.

Michelle:

I am grateful that she made it through this situation, and I'm especially grateful that she did not die at Christmas time. While it has been a rocky road, it has been a miraculous one as well. She shouldn't be here, but she is. I can feel that she is on her way to doing amazing things, and the best is yet to come. She recently called me because she was stressed out and anxious, experiencing "mom guilt" about some mundane "mistake" she felt she had made, and I am grateful for every stressed out, anxious phone call I get. Always.

Grace:

Right after Mom's stroke happened, I didn't know at all how significant or important it was. Me and my brother were hoping she'd be fine and fully come home by Christmas. They don't educate you about strokes and stuff in school. You don't really learn about it. So I didn't understand that she could be paralyzed. I didn't understand that she could be blind. No one tells you this stuff, which makes it really difficult sometimes. The only information me and my brother had was from a teacher we had in the third grade who was passionate about educating kids about things like strokes. He's the only teacher who we've ever heard say anything about it. And since Mom's stroke, we've thought about him a lot and he's someone we look up to now.

But there's definitely things since the stroke that affect us daily. I don't think our family has adjusted back to what life was like before the stroke, but maybe we've adjusted to what we might call the new normal. I mean, we're her caretakers some of the time. When Dad's not here, me and my brother make sure she eats, takes her meds, things like that. Everything that's happened still affects our lives.

Reflecting back on everything now, I can remember the year before the stroke when me and mom were really butting heads a lot. I'm a teenager, right? I always saw my mom as pretty strict, and I don't think I ever realized how lucky I was. She was saying "no" to certain things out of love, and to protect me. And after the stroke, I think I really learned to appreciate and love that part of her more than ever. I truly appreciate and am so grateful to have her as my mom now. I love you mom.

Wyatt:

I can still recall the day of the stroke, the fear and panic. I was woken up by three very loud bangs. It was 4:45am, I had no idea what was happening. I was worried, so I started to get up, but I heard the footsteps of my dad as he rushed from the couch to my parents room. I decided to wait in my room because I assumed my dad could deal with whatever was going on.

Once my dad entered the room, I clearly heard my mom,

but she didn't say a single word; she let out a weird slur of noises as she tried to speak. She was desperate and scared. Every attempt at a word had a dark, sad undertone as she grew more panicked. My first thoughts were that she may have been shot and it destroyed her brain, that would explain the banging noise. But she wouldn't be speaking if she was shot, so I quickly dismissed the idea. My mind was still on fire, a rush of thoughts going so fast that I couldn't fully identify a single one. In this flood of panic, I was still listening to the conversation between my mom and dad.

I was now standing in the middle of my room, terrified of what was going on inside of my house. I had no clue what my mom was saying, but I heard my dad and his fear. He first tried to get her to talk, questioning her to no avail. After a couple of seconds he gave up on that. I then heard him ask my mom to raise her arms. She tried to argue with him, thinking she was fine. The argument didn't achieve anything because it was just her speaking gibberish. My dad started to get very serious about it, demanding her to raise both arms. She eventually gave in and tried to raise them. Only one arm went up. That's when my dad said some of the worst words I have ever experienced, "Amber, I think you're having a stroke."

I didn't understand the significance of this at all. I had an idea of what a stroke was, but that was it.

I heard my dad call 911, I heard his conversation, I heard it all, I heard the sirens, I heard the rush of paramedics, I heard my dad argue with them because they were doubtful that my mom was having a stroke. I was standing there, frozen in fear, when my dad finally opened my door. He tells me that my mom is having a stroke, and he is going to go to the hospital.

My sister and I went to the hospital with our grandparents who live in our suite downstairs. We all hurried into the car and rushed to get there. My mind was racing, trying to process what was happening, but it couldn't do it. I believed that everything was a dream. There was no way this could be happening. It's impossible. Right?

After arriving at the hospital, we ran to where our mom was staying. I saw my dad crying outside of her room while talking to doctors. This is the only time I've ever seen him cry. The entire family was in her room. I managed to get a few words in with her before the nurses kicked us out. My dad was talking with doctors, trying to get as much information as possible. The doctors then told him that a life flight is available and my mom is being taken to a different hospital. I saw her get wheeled into a different room, my dad following closely behind.

Every family member then gathers outside of the hospital, ready to watch them be taken away to Victoria. After a few excruciating minutes, we hear the helicopter blades start to whir. The sound of the blades continued to speed up until the helicopter slowly raised off the ground. Before I knew it, the helicopter was out of sight, and I was getting into my grandparents car.

Our grandma tells us that we will have to pack our stuff when we get home because we might have to stay in Victoria for a while. I practically threw all the clothes I could find into my suitcase. My sister quickly packed clothes for her and my mom, and in a matter of minutes we were ready. We threw it all into the car and started to drive away. It was during this drive from Nanaimo to Victoria when everything started to sink in. I had roughly three hours to myself and my thoughts. As I sat there, thinking, the thought hit me. "This is real, this is actually happening."

The stroke has changed my thoughts and views so much. It shows how we take life for granted, and it all can be taken from us in seconds. The stroke was a very significant moment for the entire family, and it really changed me. My life before the stroke doesn't seem real. It has been so long since it happened. It feels like it has been an eternity, but it also seems like it was just yesterday when we were all crowded in the hospital, praying for her life. I am so grateful that she lived. I can't imagine my life without my mom.

Mike:

What happened to Amber is something I'll never forget. It's the kind of experience that is so intense that it almost feels like a dream. For a long time, I felt like I was just on autopilot, doing everything I could just to make sure our family was okay. But it wasn't easy. I've always traveled a lot for work and spent a lot of time on the road and working out of town. I never had to worry about the bills getting paid, managing the kids' schedule, or taking care of things around the house because I wasn't there. Amber always took care of things like that. But after the stroke, she couldn't do any of it. All of that responsibility was suddenly on me and I took three months off work to take care of her and the kids. It really opened my eyes.

I remember calling our bank and frantically trying to explain what had happened after her stroke. "Your mortgage isn't through us, sir," said the bank representative. "Just because you bank with us doesn't mean that your loan is held here." Eventually, I found the contact information for our mortgage broker, but that was just as frustrating. To qualify for deferred payments, they were asking me to fill out a huge forty-page PDF to show proof of what happened to Amber, which included getting documentation from the neurologist. With everything else going on, taking on all this paperwork felt like a nightmare, and I decided not to do it. I knew we'd figure out another solution, but it was challenging. Eventually, our family set up a Go-Fund-Me page to help us get by. My pride as a provider initially wasn't keen on this idea as I felt embarrassed to ask others to help. I quickly learned that it was best to put those thoughts aside and give others the chance to help us. Thank God for all the people who donated. We couldn't have done it without them.

It didn't happen all at once, but eventually, we settled into our new routine. Amber got used to being home again and was doing well in rehab. And after a few months, I started going back to work. I thought I was okay, then one day everything hit me all at once, and I had a breakdown while I was on the job. I wasn't prepared for any more stress, and found out the hard way during my first week back at work. I could feel myself getting really dizzy and light-headed, like my mind was in a fog. The guys kept asking what we should do next, and all I could muster was, "I don't know." That's when I decided to take a quick break so I could sit down for a bit. One of the managers happened to see me and asked how Amber was doing. I thought I was fine, but then I couldn't even answer him. I just broke down crying and ran out of the office.

After I took a minute to myself, I went back and found a buddy of mine. We talked for about ten minutes about what happened when I started to brush it all off and said, "Okay, it was great talking to you. I have to go back out and finish the job." My friend shook his head and said, "No, you're done. Go home. You need a break." But that's part of my mentality: bury what you're feeling way down and keep going. It was comforting for him to see the distress I was in. I listened to his advice and took the rest of the day off.

It's weird how things don't always hit you all at once. Looking back now, I don't think I ever realized how much Amber does for our family. I can honestly say that I sure appreciate her and what she does for us a whole lot more. I think the whole experience has pulled us together and re-arranged our priorities.

I used to get really stressed over things I couldn't control and worried about what other people thought of me. After the stroke, I realized none of that stuff matters. I mean, who gives a damn? This experience with Amber just knocked away all the outside noise in life. The kids have really stepped up, and I am so proud of how they've handled everything. We've all seen psychologists to learn how to come together and deal with the situation in a healthy way. And that's all thanks to Amber.

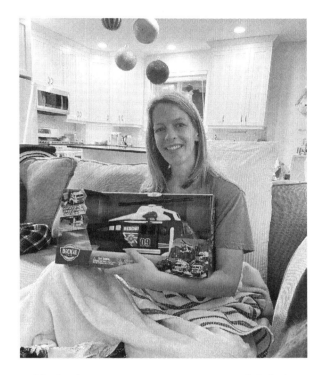

My Strokeaversary present, my very own life flight.

January 29th 2022, first family walk longer than 10 minutes.

Chapter 5

The Purpose of Life

Struggling

When you feel you continue to come up against the same wall over and over, you need to see it for what it is.

You are at the point in your life where you are on the precipice of mastering a lesson you have been working on.

You are not being punished or doing something wrong.

You are not being left alone to flounder around and suffer.

Your guides and higher self are trying to lovingly let you know the answer to the lessons you are learning.

You would never take a huge exam without studying; it is the same with life lessons.

Practice makes progress, because perfect does not exist.

So take the time to be grateful for the lesson you are working through.

Try not to fight the process, but rather ponder what your focus should be.

You have the strength to learn and grow, recognize that, dwell on that.

You are stronger than you think.

ONE OF THE questions I'm left with now is, "Why am I here, and why does it suck so bad?" The truth is, life isn't supposed to be easy. On the Other Side, there is only love, contentment, and peace. Our souls come here to learn everything else, things like patience, caregiving, empathy, forgiveness, mediation, pain, guilt, shame, anger, regret, and much more. Earth sometimes is just one really hard, shitty school. It's the type of place souls come to for deep transformation, unbelievable growth, and the full experience of what it's like to be human.

If you've ever asked yourself why you're here or what your life purpose might be, I want you to know that you are already fulfilling it just by being alive. Just by breathing. This may sound overly simplistic, but it's true. Many of us have been conditioned to associate the words 'life purpose' with a specific job or career path. But our souls look at purpose quite differently. Our souls, which exist as infinite beings of energy, contain the essence of who we are. We continually seek new ways to learn, grow, and evolve. And the number one way to grow is by experiencing life. For many of us, this may mean walking through a human experience, although our soul can create life in any single dimension or in multiple dimensions all at the same time. It's hard to wrap our human minds around things like this. How can you explain things that don't have a human definition?

What makes it even more fascinating is that each soul plans their life before they are born. Some people refer to this life plan as a "soul contract," although I'm personally not a fan of that term. I like to think of it more like a fluid plan outlining all the "classes" we want to take on Earth school. Purposely planned with plenty of wiggle room for free will and unexpected changes. We create this plan with full awareness of everything that has happened in the past and will happen in the future. As a soul, you know everything and have access to all the information that has ever or will ever exist. You are able to see all possible outcomes of any given decision and the benefit or fallout of any given scenario. You use your soul's infinite knowledge to plan a human life that will allow you to make the most out of your experience.

When your soul is in the planning phase and ready to go

back to "school" it's a little like walking up to a huge buffet, but instead of the trays being filled with food, they are filled with life lessons. The soul views these lessons as learning opportunities which can help us expand our consciousness and understanding of all living things. These lessons or plans may include what we do for a living, but also incorporate all aspects of our personal lives, romantic relationships, friendships, health challenges, emotional ups and downs, traumatic events, and more.

So your soul walks down this "buffet line," and it scoops up a little bit of this lesson and a little bit of that lesson and a huge heaping bit of that one over there. Once it reaches the end, your soul shows your spirit guides what it picked and asks them what they think. Your spirit guides always offer feedback with love and the intention of helping you make the best life plan possible. They might say something like, "We don't think you'll survive that heaping part. Let's put some back." Or maybe, "We know your soul could handle a little more of this, so let's add to that." So, you add some and you take some off until you have your perfect plate. There are also specific guides whose sole focus is life planning, so they will be beside you offering their sage advice as you walk through this phase. By the end, your soul has the whole thing planned with a solid understanding of what will happen throughout your entire lifetime.

Through it all, everything is done with love, never malice. By the time your soul finishes picking out its lessons, it's likely thinking, "This is what I'm going to do in this life, and I have so much support." Nothing is given to you as a punishment or something bad like, "Oh, you're a shitty soul, so you get eighteen scoops of this one crappy thing. Have fun trying to survive." It truly feels more like an empowering message of yes, you can do this. You are strong, you are capable, and you're wise enough now to survive this.

For instance, when I was on the Other Side, I learned that one of the lessons I'm learning is patience. My guides told me after my stroke, I'd have to learn a lifetime of patience in a very short time period of eighteen months. Patience is something that I've struggled with my whole life and I can see why my soul might have chosen it. But most of us won't know what our lessons are once we're in human form. We're not meant to know. However, if you're curious, you can probably look at the themes playing out in your life to get clues. One theme I see a lot with people is the caregiving lesson. You can almost always tell when someone has signed up to learn about caregiving because they'll struggle with boundaries and burn themselves out trying to help everyone else while neglecting their own needs. It doesn't always have to be that, though. Your soul might want to learn other lessons that revolve around experiences of guilt, regret, loss, anger, self-worth, or empathy. The options are endless. No matter what lessons you have, it's about learning to walk through it or carry it with you for the rest of your life.

Also, your soul or higher self will never pick just one. They often will pick multiple lessons that can be changed, combined, or altered depending on how our life unfolds. As we learn and grow, so does our soul. It's all interconnected. The purpose is to experience the full gambit of what it means to be human—the good, the bad, and the ugly. We want it all. The beauty of it is, there is no doing it wrong. As we walk through these lives, there is no pass/fail mentality from the Other Side. There is no gold star or perfect score. That's just not how it works. Everything is simply viewed as valuable learning experiences completely devoid of judgment.

Having this awareness can help us understand why certain things happen, but it also doesn't necessarily make it easier to experience. Life is hard. I don't think living your purpose means you're happy all the time. It's exactly the opposite. Purpose can be painful. It can be hard. It can be infuriating. It can feel so agonizing. But it's still your purpose at that moment. If everything in life was perfect, we'd never grow. We'd never learn.

After all, the true definition of enlightenment is being able to walk through every human emotion and every human experience so we may gain an innate understanding of what it feels like. Our goal when we plan a life is not only to focus on achieving joy; that's only one part of enlightenment. Enlightenment from your soul's perspective means that you have walked through every possible scenario—to experience what it's like to be rich, poor, loved, hated, successful, defeated, everything. And a part of that is feeling every emotion under the sun too. We're here to feel pleasure and anger, pride and guilt, friendship and resentment, happiness and sadness, companionship and loneliness, love and betrayal, and more. And in an effort to achieve enlightenment, our soul makes a plan that will help us confront a myriad of human interactions.

I think it's important to distinguish that it's our souls that choose this, not our human selves. Our soul makes the plan, and as humans, we simply walk through it. That doesn't mean that you have to go through everything alone. Your soul is always connected to you in every moment of your life. It's always tuned in and doesn't take breaks. Picture it as just a little piece of you. If your soul were a raincloud, you would be the raindrop. And right now, if you were to beam yourself to the Other Side, your soul would look just like you. You would feel like yourself. Just a more expanded, all-encompassing form of your true essence.

After hearing this, some people might be thinking, "Okay, if my soul is planning all this stuff out, do I really have free will?" And I can confidently say yes. While our souls do the planning, they leave room for different pathways and different choices. It's kind of like those Choose Your Own Adventure books from childhood. You start with a fluid plan and a starting point, and from there it's like a roadmap with all of these potential pathways you could take. As you go along your journey and things get too hard or too easy, or if something unexpectedly changes and alters your plans, five other paths will appear. So, if something prevents you from going down the most likely path or you don't want to take it, there are always alternatives. The possibilities are endless.

Most of the time, we tend to go down the path our soul chose for us. When this path appears in life, we innately have a gut instinct that tells us to go in that direction. Most of the time we'll say something like, "Oh, okay, this looks like a good choice." But every once in a while, we grow, we work on ourselves, or something outside of us happens to influence our choices and we'll go in a different way. As a human, the thought of deviating from our plans might make us nervous or anxious, but it's not like that for your soul. Your soul is always observing and can predict what will happen. They're never rattled by things like this. So if a change does happen, more often than not they are thinking to themselves, "Oh, okay. She went this way, so now the most likely way to reach the next step is by doing this, so we'll plan accordingly."

As we make choices and walk down different pathways, other beings of energy called spirit guides are paying attention too. Spirit guides are souls who have lived many, many human lives and have evolved spiritually to a point where they no longer incarnate. Instead, they dedicate their time to helping other humans walk through their lives, offering love, support, and guidance. Your spirit guides chose you and you chose your spirit guides. You were brought together both because you felt a connection and also because they felt they had the experience to help you get through the life lessons your soul chose. If your soul chose to walk through the experience of grief and loss, for example, one or more of your guides probably lost a spouse or someone very close to them in one of their past lives and feels called to help you through that.

The number of guides you connect with is going to depend on you and your unique life plan. The average number is two or three. My spirit guides are Jessica, Gayle, and Peter. Jessica looks like a twenty-one-year-old blonde bombshell. She's very outgoing and an outspoken performer. Anytime I've done live events or streamed videos, she's always there. I think of her as the fun friend who comes out when I'm working. She loves it when people ask her questions and enjoys talking about all the things that make us human. Many times, she'll sing answers to uncomfortable questions instead of speaking because she thinks it makes what she's saying more palatable (she's hilarious). She also loves animals and is always there when I communicate with them. Jessica's just such a ball of energy, and everybody loves her.

Gayle is more my dominant guide, and her energy feels like the wisest, most loving grandma you've ever known. She always knows what to say, and I can always count on her to encourage me and offer me support as I walk through this crazy human experience. I get quite a bit of anxiety sometimes, and she helps me focus on the lessons and stay on track with my goals. She's there with me when I meditate and is always looking to help ground and center me. I've noticed that she's very interested in my healing gifts, too, and wants to help me develop them. Gayle takes special interest in people going through loss and will often sit with humans offering support as they grieve. Both Jessica and Gayle love to visit people who are watching my live videos and help them on their spiritual journey.

My third guide is an energy made up of the highest collective consciousness. When I first became aware of their presence, I didn't know what to call them, so I named them Peter. The energy they give off is very empowering and strong, yet they are completely genderless and do not appear in human form. I associate them with the color green. Peter is not particularly concerned with the day-to-day of human living, but is very interested in helping with the enlightenment of all humankind. When Peter talks, it's very measured, slow, and to the point. They often use words I usually don't use. Peter doesn't stay around all the time the same way Jessica and Gayle do; they only come in when they feel it's really needed. I always know it's Peter because I'll start yawning. They almost come into my body, and their thoughts become my words.

Because I'm spiritually gifted with the ability to communicate with the Other Side, a lot of people ask me, "If you can see and talk with your guides, why don't you ask them everything?" The truth is, when I'm not working, I rarely interact with them at all. It's only when I'm struggling that I ask my guides to be there and express gratitude that I don't have to walk through this life alone. We aren't meant to rely on them to make all of our choices in life. Many people will never directly communicate with their spirit guides, and there is nothing wrong with that. We are meant to figure things out for ourselves. Hearing this might feel hard, but it's the truth, even for me. Our souls planned these lives with complete faith that we could do it. And we can.

Throughout it all, your spirit guides stay with you to offer love, encouragement, and support. Usually, they are there silently walking beside you and celebrating your ability to be human. They are your biggest supporters, but much like a parent teaching their child to walk, they want you to learn how to overcome challenges and learn new things on your own. They see how strong you are, how much you've been through, and wholeheartedly believe in your ability to keep going, even when life gets hard.

They won't change things, but will help us see the different directions we could take in a subtle way. It's not like in the movies where they come crashing in and say, "Go this way!" Or "Go that way!" What you'll feel is more of a gentle energy surrounding you to help you move forward or make a choice, whatever it may be. For many people, this will come through like a gut feeling or intuition.

Sometimes, we are given these gut feelings before we understand what they mean. Our guides are endlessly patient and know that it often takes several opportunities or nudges to get us to listen and there is nothing wrong with that. As humans, we need time to process information and learn our lessons– it's a natural part of life. So, don't be too hard on yourself if you feel like you haven't made as much progress as you'd hoped, or if you're being faced with the same issues or problems over and over again. It just means that you are deep within the learning. Be kind to yourself, and remember that you're exactly where you are meant to be.

Your spirit guides will never leave you. They will never let you down. They are just gently nudging us in the best way for soul growth. It's not always what we expect. Sometimes your guides might see you walking toward something really difficult and really challenging, and encourage you to do it anyway because it's such a great learning opportunity. Here's a common example: Let's say you are curious about pursuing a new job but aren't sure whether to go for it. Eventually, you decide to take the leap, so you quit your comfy job and start a position at a brand new company. Once you start, you realize that you're working for a narcissistic boss who is pushing you so hard you quickly reach your breaking point. Or maybe after a few weeks, you get fed up with your co-workers who are driving you crazy. Your human self may be wondering why the hell you were guided in the direction of such a horrible new job. But your spirit guides nudged you that way because your soul needed and wanted to learn those lessons. Good and bad don't exist from their perspective. It's all just different levels of learning.

When I hear people say, "Gosh, I just want my guide's

opinion," sometimes I tell them that it's better to go with your own human preference. Your guides will always push you toward the path of most learning. Full stop. And sometimes, as humans, we just need a break to relax a bit, which is totally okay. You're not missing an opportunity by going against what your guides say. What's meant for you will never pass you by. Instead, by doing what you want, you're sending a message to the universe that sounds more like, "You know what, I'm going to pass on those huge lessons right now. I'm just going to focus over here where it is a little bit easier."

When your guides hear that, they won't be upset. They aren't like harsh teachers in school that are here to scold or correct us. They'll never point out what we did wrong or insist we do something over again because we failed the first time. In their eyes, failure doesn't exist. They always approach us from a place of genuine love and understanding. If they see you decline an opportunity or choose something different from what they nudged you toward, they aren't judging you. More often than not, they are thinking, "Oh, her human body is tired. Let's lead her in this direction or give her a few signs that everything is going to be okay."

And when you're ready to take on challenges in life? Your

guides will be right there with you. They won't protect you from all the things you might deem as hard though. They approach your journey more like a parent would. For instance, I know I've equipped my kids to walk through the life they created. I'm also here to give them a cuddle and a word of encouragement when they are really struggling. I'm not going to do it for them, but I am going to embrace them in my arms and say, "You know what? This is hard, but you've got this. You are strong, and I know you are capable of wrapping your head around what you're struggling with and coming up with solutions." Our spirit guides are like that. They offer us comfort that feels like a warm hug from a loving parent.

So live your life. Have faith in yourself. When things go wrong, go easy on yourself. We're not meant to be perfect all the time. We're here to make mistakes. No matter what happens, we're meant to experience it all. There is no such thing as pass/fail in life. There is no judgment. No reward. No punishment. No "You could have done this." Or "You should have done that." Nothing like that at all. Not even a hint. Pass/fail and reward/punishment are a human construct. It doesn't belong to your soul.

Chapter 6
Reincarnation and Our Soul's Journey

Joy

If you take the time, you surely will see.
Joy and abundance strain to break free.
The sun ever shines, warmth kisses your face.
A friend forgives, with passion and grace.
A soft wind whispers, touching your skin.
A baby gifts you with their very first grin.
The Earth is not sad, she does not cry.
She celebrates and glorifies both you and I.
Please open your eyes, mind, soul, and heart.
Feel the freedom we have received from the start.
Do not miss the gifts we can access each day.
Meditate, celebrate, love hard, and pray.
We are not so different, believe it is true.
Coming together is long overdue.
Gratitude, joy, connection, and love.
Many lessons we often miss from above.
Take time, smell the roses, say hello, don't walk by.
Try to see yourself in a stranger's kind eye.
Take a breath, sing a song, dance madly, love true.
Realize innate joy and gratitude is in you.
Go easy on yourself, forgive and forget.
Practice patience, no one is perfect just yet.
Remember these words as you move through your day.
Meditate, celebrate, love hard, and pray.

MANY OF US are familiar with the word reincarnation and the spiritual concept that our souls, after biological death, begin a new life in a new body. I actually dislike that concept because it implies that we plan a life, come here, live our life, die, go back to the Other Side, take stock, and then do it all over again. The whole idea revolves around a linear timeline, which might make sense to our human brain, but in my experience, that's not how it works.

When I had my NDE and went to the Other Side, I experienced a higher energy, a presence that was overseeing everything with love. I call it God, you might call it something else. The name is not important. What I experienced had no face, had no human form. It simply emanated from everything and everyone, every animal, every part of nature, everything I could see or feel. All life is created by this God energy and everything is intrinsically connected to it. And as God creates life, it also gives our higher selves the ability to create life too.

Our higher selves love every part of this. There are certain things we're not able to experience on the Other Side, and exploring different lifetimes allows us to learn, grow, and become more enlightened beings. It's the ultimate way to get closer to that God energy. So our higher selves plan lives, usually multiple lives at a time.

Each human life that is created by the higher self is a different person, living in a different part of the world, having a different human experience. And our higher selves continuously create human life with the intention of experiencing all that life has to offer, in every way possible. And because time and space don't exist on the Other Side, each of these lives is playing out simultaneously, regardless of what time period they may be living in—the past, present, and future. Some even exist in other dimensions. Each life exists independently in and of itself but is still interconnected.

I like to compare it to a water cycle. Imagine our higher selves are like rain clouds on the Other Side. They are continuously producing raindrops (human lives) and as the human lives end, they evaporate and return to the cloud (higher self.) It's a very circular process that is ongoing and never-ending. There is no waiting period for one life to end before the next one begins. Each of the lives our highest self created is playing out at the exact same time.

When a human life ends, we are reunited with our other lives, our higher self, and with God. When we cross over to the Other Side, we never really die. We just continue living in a different form and are surrounded with love. There is no voice of judgment that says, "Oh, you did really good." Or, "Now you get to go and either be rewarded or punished for what you did or didn't do." That's not at all what happens. There is no tally system. Life is simply learning. Our higher self continues creating lives because we want to, not because we're forced to or because we did something wrong. We love learning and view life as the best way to grow. When we come back to the Other Side we share what we learned in life, and by doing this it contributes something sacred to our higher selves, which then contributes to the highest collective energy. We are all working toward enlightenment, and we're doing it together.

One of the ways we share is by participating in what's known as a life review. I like to think of it as sitting around a table with your spirit guides and that highest God energy. Your entire life plays out, almost like a movie on a screen. As you watch, you get to see how your life unfolded, not just from your point of view, but from the point of view of everyone you came into contact with. For instance, let's say that when you were in your twenties, you had a huge argument with a friend. After that argument, you kinda forgot about it and moved on. But that friend still remembered your comment, and it really knocked their confidence and triggered something within them that they struggled with for a long time. During your life review, you would be able to see that experience through their eyes.

As this life review is taking place, it's all done with love. There is no judgment. It's not like your guides are sitting there saying, "Oh, you said this horrible thing, and it really affected them." It's more like, "Oh, okay. This was my view of that. But wow, there was a whole other part to this." There are no pointing fingers. It is only picking out lessons that you may not have been able to see as a human. The truth is, most of the time, humans have no idea how we're affecting people's lives. Even if we're good people who genuinely try to do the right thing, we're not mind readers (okay, maybe I kind of am.) But it's impossible to see everything. The life review shows us all of it. We can see our entire life and the lives of every other person.

In some situations, people might cross over to the Other Side without participating in a life review right away. This is common if you experience a very long, painful death that involves harsh circumstances like terminal illness, murder, or something else that was really horrific. In cases like this, your soul gets a break when the human life ends. I like to think of it like going to a spa, but in reality it's a lot more like floating in peaceful blackness while your soul recuperates. Complete blackness might not sound peaceful, but it is to your soul. It gives us a chance to heal before we transition and start our life review.

This place of healing darkness is also what you might consider a holding place for many people who experience NDEs. It's not uncommon to hear stories where humans describe seeing only blackness or darkness when they die (or almost die.) It's because they were in this "soul spa" where they had a chance to separate and shed the weight of the heavy human body– even if it was just for a little while– in order to keep them alive.

Whether you go straight to the life review, or take a pit

stop at the "soul spa" first, it doesn't matter. Either journey is okay and neither one is better or worse than the other. Eventually we all experience our life review and transition fully to the Other Side where we merge back with our higher selves. We continue our existence and continue to support and love one another, even those who are still living on Earth.

I've seen this firsthand when I practice mediumship and channel people's deceased loved ones. They often come through with love and knowledge of what's going on in our life. They always appear in physical form, the way we remember them. It's not like TV, where if they die in a horrific car crash, they come through bleeding and broken. They always look beautiful, like the best version of their human selves. All of the people we care about are always there for us, overseeing things and sending love. You will 100% see your loved ones again, without a doubt. And your pets are there with them too.

Hearing this point of view about dying and the afterlife might be hard for some to understand, and that's okay. As humans, we're not meant to understand everything. But for our souls, it makes all the sense in the world. Each life is as purpose-filled as the next one.

Chapter 7

Have Faith, We Are Not Alone

Faith

Faith, such a simple word, yet at times it feels so unattainable
Have Faith they say, those who do not know what it is to be me.
Faith in what, I ask? Who or what is worthy of my Faith?
Shall I place it upon some unknown? Give it to a God?
Where does Faith belong? Within myself?
The answers to these questions ever provoke thought.
Faith is not palpable, cannot grant one instant satisfaction.
So why then, do we place so much value on its presence?
Such a simple word yet can help a soul grow.
Faith means we can trust in ourselves.
We can know without doubt that we are not alone.
No matter where you choose to place your Faith,
It will help to raise you up.
A human without Faith, is as a heart without a beat
Beautiful and perfect in its existence, but purposeless.
So, I will say to you, have Faith.
Faith that you can take this life to amazing places.
Faith that you are beautiful and perfect in your existence,
Faith to strengthen your purpose.
It will ignite your soul, bring you back into balance.
Remind you of a time long forgotten, when
you honored your connection
To all living things.
Have Faith you are not alone, as your heart beats so too does your
Ever growing soul.
Faith, although a simple word, is not so simple to comprehend.
Trust your soul to lead the way to true Faith.
Know that with Faith, you will never truly be lost.

THROUGHOUT TIME, FAITH has carried the weight of religion. For thousands of years, people in society have been raised from a young age to have faith in God and the teachings of their church. Most religious doctrines were created to help people find hope and a sense of purpose in their human existence, which can be really beautiful. But religion doesn't always tell the whole story.

In my own life, I went from being intensely religious to feeling very angry with religion to curious about spirituality over the course of decades. Faith was something I'd always struggled with, maybe because I had no faith in myself when I was younger. I didn't know what was wrong with me or why I was so different from everyone else. Once I decided to have faith in something—for me it was God, Jesus, and the Holy Spirit—it didn't necessarily make it any easier. I just felt judged by the people around me who told me I was constantly doing it wrong.

For a long time, I was taught that in order to be a good Christian I had to go to church, follow the rules, pay my tithes, and volunteer to be worthy. You see, I used to be a born again Christian, and if you didn't follow their path, your ability to get into heaven was affected. This never sat right with me. I mean, what if you live in an area of the world where you aren't exposed to many other people and have never heard the word "Christian" because it's not talked about? Are all those people going to hell because they haven't been exposed to these beliefs? I don't think that's reality and it's something I struggled with for years.

After the church turned me away when I came out as a psychic, my faith did a complete 180. I started to have faith in myself and the human process. I started to cultivate faith in my guides and the Other Side as a whole. I know I am capable of living this life and achieving what I'm meant to achieve. For a long time, I had held this blind faith in my heart, but when I had my stroke and saw the Other Side, it solidified everything.

When I crossed over, I felt that highest God energy and there was no condemnation or judgment. There was no one sitting behind a desk banging a gavel and demanding that I needed to make amends or ask for forgiveness for my sins. There was none of that. I only experienced an overwhelming, unconditional love. When you get there someday, you will be greeted with love too. You will be seen for who you really are and embraced and celebrated for all the learning you've contributed to the collective. The Other Side is our home and Earth is our school. Each of us is here for a reason and the part you're playing is an important one. You are truly making more of a difference than you might realize. Your religious beliefs (or lack thereof) will never affect that in a negative way.

After that experience, I've stopped associating myself with one particular spiritual community (although I'll never judge anyone who does–I believe everyone is empowered to choose what's right for them.) I guess you could say that I'm the most spiritual, non-spiritual person on the planet. I'm not new-age. I don't read horoscopes. I don't pay attention to astrology. I don't read tarot cards. I have some crystals, but I don't use them. And I'm allergic to sage. I have a Bible beside me while I work because I think it brings together a lot of humans and I see a lot of value and beauty in the lessons it teaches. I also follow a lot of people who are Jewish because their sense of community is so inspiring. The Amish are a group I admire because of how connected they are and how well they look after one another. I also really resonate with Buddhism, faiths that encourage us to connect with nature, and a plethora of other beliefs. My faith is all-encompassing. I truly believe that at the end of it all, we will all be celebrated for rocking this human thing, and if that is all we strive for, that is good enough.

The only thing I don't resonate with is the judgment part of any belief system. Sometimes people become so dedicated to one religion that they end up judging others who don't agree with their faith. This mentality can create division because not all of humanity is going to believe the same thing. What we believe has so much to do with how we were raised, our personal life experiences, and what we feel called to connect with in this life. When we condemn others who don't think the way we think or believe what we believe, it's often rooted in fear. And fear makes us crazy and anxious. Creating fear about how we live, how we think, or how we feel—I can't get behind that.

Just imagine for a moment that you attend a church, and they are discussing the topic of sexuality. For argument's sake, let's just say your sexuality or gender are fluid, or maybe you'd prefer not to identify with one thing in particular, or maybe you don't know yet, and it's something you're struggling with. Now let's say the pastor finds out and they say something like, "You know what, you just have to ask for forgiveness and stop being attracted to the same sex." At that moment, you're thinking, "Oh my God. What if I am attracted to the same sex? If I don't listen to these people, I'm going to hell." In that scenario, how would you feel? You probably wouldn't be able to stop worrying about it, which is unfortunate because you're being led by fear. I think that any concept that implies that if one person doesn't fit the mold, they will live in eternal punishment is horrible.

So what do you do in a scenario like that? Live in fear that someone is going to find out about your sexuality and declare that you're a terrible person? Do you continue participating in a community that rejects you if you don't fit into what they believe is acceptable? Too many people find themselves in this situation and they are left with the impression that they don't belong and there's nowhere for them to go. It's not right. As a society, we have to do better. Why not celebrate people for who they are?

If you're reading this and you resonate with feeling like an outcast, have lost faith, or are struggling to find something to believe in, I want you to know that you're not alone. Don't lose hope. You don't have to have faith in the world all the time. I know so many things are messed up right now. You don't have to have faith in a God. You don't have to have faith in spirituality or a religion unless you want to. Just have faith that you are capable of walking through life, no matter how hard it gets, because you are enough exactly as you are. Even if you struggle to believe in yourself, don't give up. You can do this. I know it's hard. The world is thrown at us constantly, and it's not always easy to know what to do when everything feels chaotic and out of control. But you are stronger and more powerful than you realize. Have faith that you planned this life perfectly in all its imperfections because you knew you were strong enough to live it. If you're having an especially tough time, focus on the spiritual lessons because I guarantee they're really good right now. You're growing and evolving more than you know.

On your journey, there will be people to help you, and it's okay to seek clarity and ask for help. Just be cautious and use your judgment when choosing who to go to for assistance. Try not to give your power away and rely too much on others for every decision.

As humans, we often seek answers and a clear path forward telling us what to do and how to do it. We want this because it provides us with a sense of safety and security. We think that if we know all the answers, we can protect ourselves from getting hurt or having things go wrong. Feelings of uncertainty or ambiguity can be really hard, so when we're feeling lost it's not uncommon to seek counsel from someone outside of ourselves. While seeking guidance is totally understandable, it can be a slippery slope if it's done in an unhealthy way.

I remember one woman who came to me years ago after her husband had committed suicide. It was a heart wrenching situation. She had been paying to see another psychic medium every month for the last ten years so she could stay in touch with him. By the time she decided to come to me, she explained that she was facing a very difficult choice. Her new boyfriend had proposed, and she wanted to ask her late husband for permission. So I tapped into the Other Side and the first thing I channeled from her husband was, "This needs to be the last medium you go to." I felt bad saying it, but her deceased husband was very clear. He said, "I love you and will always be near you, but you need to live your life." He'd been trying to get this message to her for years, but the other psychic medium wouldn't say it because they wanted to keep making money off of her. It's so unfortunate because it's an area where people can really take advantage.

Don't get me wrong, there are spiritual intuitives, healers, and psychics out there who are genuine and really want to help. If you find someone like that and you feel like you can trust them, I think that's wonderful. I would just recommend not letting yourself become overly reliant on them. Sometimes getting a psychic reading can create unintended consequences. For example, let's say you're studying for a really important exam and you've spent hours preparing for it, but you know you still have a little bit of work to do. You're a bit nervous, so you decide to hire a psychic to see what they think. So you ask them, "Am I going to pass the exam?" And the psychic says, "Yes, you'll pass." You leave the reading confident that you're going to do well, so maybe you get a little lazy and stop studying. And because of your free will decisions, the narrative changes, and you don't pass the test after all. That doesn't mean that the psychic got it wrong, but nothing in life is set in stone. We all can change the course of our lives at any moment, and it is up to each of us to trust our inner knowing to guide us toward the right choices for us.

And because I care about you, I'm going to tell you something else: always beware if a healer or psychic tells you, "Come to me every week, and I'll take care of everything for you." That's a red flag. You don't need readings constantly and certainly don't need to feel pressured to pay for an expensive course for someone to tell you how to do life better. You are capable of making every decision. You have everything inside of you to do it on your own. If you do go to someone for a little extra support, make sure to vet them first.

Chapter 8

Help and Healing from Your Guides

Thrive

This world tells us to be strong, stand alone.
We must achieve success with strength on our own.
Be an island, a star, shine as bright as you can.
Don't look back, focus forward, have goals, set a plan.
It all sounds so easy, yet we suffer great pain.
So many strong people cry rivers like rain.
This world tells each person they are doing it wrong.
If we cannot thrive in chaos, then we are not strong.
Do not believe it, there is no badge to be won.
By suffering in silence, until life is done.
Draw close to your family, your friends, and your foe.
Find your village, your people, and soon you will know.
There is strength in numbers, you are not alone.
In the many who love you, you can find a new home
Society is wrong. It is speaking great lies.
You can see it in so many humans' sad eyes.
We are lonely, distraught, and suffering despair.
We feel we are owed it because life is not fair.
Hear me when I speak, you are surrounded in love.
From your family, your friends and guides up above.
So if you're feeling despair, one lone shining light.
Know there is strength in numbers, you can win the fight.

A S HUMAN BEINGS, we are constantly exchanging energy with our environment and those around us. Every interaction we have, every place we go, and every thought we think creates an energetic imprint on our entire body. Some of this energy can be positive and uplifting, while other energy can be negative and draining.

Negative energy can come from a variety of sources, like stress from daily life, burnout on the job, and misunderstandings or arguments with the people around us, just to name a few. Over time, the negative energy accumulates. Unless we find a way to clear and release it, it sits with us, slowly deteriorating our quality of life.

This is why it's so important to learn how to cleanse and protect yourself. It can be a powerful way to release energetic blockages, negative emotions, unwanted thoughts, and promote a sense of calm and clarity. Not only that, but emotional cleansing can be a very healing spiritual practice which can help facilitate a stronger connection with your guides, your higher self, and your connection to the Other Side.

What I'm sharing with you now is my own cleanse and protect ritual that I've changed and adapted over the years. I intentionally keep it flexible and changeable so you can customize it depending on what your circumstances are. Feel free to use this as a guide, practice with it, and make it your own.

To begin, I usually sit with my back straight and legs uncrossed, with my palms face up. It's helpful to put a selenite crystal in one or both of your hands. Selenite is a self-cleansing crystal and magnifies the work you're doing. Bonus points if you have both of your feet on the floor. Doing this helps you ground to the earth's energy, anchoring yourself to the present moment.

Next, to help your body relax, you're going to do the 4-7-8 breathing technique. It's something you can do anytime, anywhere, and can be especially helpful when you're feeling stressed or anxious. It works by slowing your breathing down and inducing calm and relaxation from the inside out.

Start by inhaling for a count of four, holding your breath for a count of seven, and exhaling for a count of eight. As you inhale, visualize breathing in vibrant white light and loving energy from your spirit guides and the Other Side. And when you exhale, visualize breathing out any negativity, heaviness, or human yuck that you might be carrying around. If you find it difficult to hold your breath, you can start by holding it for a shorter amount of time and gradually work your way up. You can repeat this as many times as you'd like. I usually do it between three and five times.

After you've finished the breathing exercise, you can read this out loud or silently to yourself:

Supreme Being, all that is. Thank you for the opportunity to connect with you during this time in my life. May I be guided by your love and light. Surround me with your golden divine energy. Only the most pure, positive, highest energy essence is allowed in this space. Teachers, angels, spirit guides, loved ones, guiding energies, thank you all for coming. I intend accurate, open, clear lines of communication. Amen.

If the prayer doesn't suit you, feel free to adapt it to your liking. Maybe instead of Supreme Being you'd prefer to say God or Mother Nature. That's okay too. Feel free to expand or shorten it as much as you'd like. This is about making this prayer/meditation something that resonates with you and makes you feel supported and loved.

Now you can set your intentions for the next steps. For instance, anytime I host an event or do a reading for someone, I always ask for that person to be touched by what's being offered, for it to be a life-changing experience, and for them to feel even a small amount of what I feel every day from my guides. If that person is experiencing any physical, emotional, or relationship discomfort, for that to be cleansed, healed, and soothed too. After I set my intentions, I close with a cleanse and protection prayer that sounds something like this:

Please cleanse me of anything not serving a positive purpose and protect me from picking up and carrying with me anything that will not serve me well.

Once you get to this step, you can ask your spirit guides to come through silently or out loud, using whatever words feel natural to you. I usually let them know that I am open to receiving guidance and I request for the information to come through to me clearly, concisely, and without confusion. Connecting to your spirit guides is a deeply personal and individual process, and there is no right or wrong way to do it. You can simply let them know what's going on and tell them why you're seeking their help.

I remember a time in my life when I used to have so much hip pain that it would make my daily walk completely miserable. It was hard, because my daily walk was not just a part of my routine, but something that had become very important for my mental and physical health. Not being able to do it was really taking a toll on me. So I asked my guides to give me a break and to take it away, even if it was just for that day.

I knew at the time that the issue with my hip was probably something I needed to go to physical therapy for, and there were things I could do to make it better, but I put it off and put it off. I recognized I could probably have done more to take care of it and I took responsibility, but sometimes my guides would help relieve the pain for a little while. So, I did the 4-7-8 breathing and cleanse and protect prayers. I told them that I knew it was my responsibility to take care of my body, but I really needed their help so I could find some relief. I wanted to be able to walk and practice my own self-care so I could have the energy to help other people. And they heard me. Even though they weren't able to magically cure me or take away the problems in my hips, they did help me find strength and I experienced a break from the discomfort that was causing me so much pain.

If you desperately need relief, you can ask your guides for a break too. Let them know what's going on and be honest about how you're feeling. Let's say, for example, that you are suffering from insomnia and want to be able to sleep through the night. You can ask your guides to help alleviate your symptoms so you can sleep until 7:00 am the next day. Let them know that if they do this for you, that you will commit to taking time to think about the reasons why you're struggling. You can do this with the intention of finding the underlying cause or planning ways to find treatment. Think of this exchange with your guides as a little bit of a give and take. At the end of it all, it's important to honor your promise to them and find that time for reflection because if you don't, it sends a not-so-great message. They will never punish you, but they may send you reminders to try and resolve things on your own.

After all, your spirit guides are here for a purpose: to guide you. They stand beside you unwaveringly without any judgment. But they won't fix or solve all the issues in life. Your spirit guides want to help you, but also want to empower you to help yourself. So, asking them to help with every small inconvenience in life, like the common cold or sitting in rush hour traffic, may not get much of a response.

However, during the moments when you've reached your breaking point and you feel like you just can't handle it anymore, yes, ask them for relief and they will 100% be there. Sometimes we have to walk through really shitty experiences and we don't always understand why. But most of the time the answer is simple: your human self didn't choose any of this, but your soul did. Your spirit guides would never want to interfere with your soul plan, even if it's painful or uncomfortable.

If you're experiencing something bigger and more permanent like chronic disease, cancer, abuse, trauma, anxiety, depression, or anything like that, it can feel really hard. Your spirit guides can't cure it or completely take it away, but they can help you find hope. They can help you picture a time when that pain will no longer be there, making it a bit easier to endure what you're going through. They will always be by your side and will never abandon you.

Asking for help from spirit guides is something that anyone can do. It doesn't matter if you consider yourself to be spiritual or not, no matter if you practice energetic work, or if you've ever interacted with your spirit guides before. All you need is faith that asking for help will work.

Trust me, I know how profoundly difficult it is to have faith when life throws its worst at you. I know how hard it can be to be human. When life is crappy, it's so much more difficult to have faith. So you don't have to have 100% faith for this work. You don't have to have 100% belief in everything I'm saying. You just need to have a small piece of your heart that tells you things can be better than what they are. As you start to see results and see that your guides are there for you, your faith will just naturally grow, even if it's just a little bit.

But healing will never work if you don't believe in it. Your mind is extremely powerful and can influence what happens more than we know. Just like believing you'll get sick can make you unwell, fixating on a thought or thing only brings more of your attention to it. So, faith is important, and it's hard. But I know you are fully capable of cultivating it.

As you're moving forward, if you don't know your guides, you can focus on mine. A lot of people who follow me on social media or take my workshops have gotten to know my guides and find it helpful to concentrate on them as higher energetic beings who are there to support them. If you do that, your guides will show up too. They will all show up. My guides aren't just for me. They're here to help all of us and will come forward whenever you call on them. There will never be a time when they don't. Your guides and my guides are always with us. You are never alone.

Cleanse

Just as the rain cleanses the Earth, our tears cleanse our souls.

When life is too heavy, too sad, unbearable, exhausting,
frustrating, or just too much, allow yourself a moment.

Give yourself permission to be vulnerable and to feel.

Allow your tears to cleanse and release all of your pent up energy.

Some may see letting go and shedding those tears
as a weakness. Just as rain brings new life to this
Earth, so too can tears if you let them.

They can allow you to let go of all of life's heaviness, they
can cleanse your soul unlike anything else we experience,
and once that is done there is room for endless growth.

I've created this next section specifically for people who identify as psychics, intuitives, and healers, and the ones who practice energetic work on themselves and on others. What follows is a description of how I cleanse and protect myself before I do readings or healings. I want to share it with you so you feel supported as you go about doing this important work in the world.

To begin, I find a comfortable position–sitting or standing—and visualize an iridescent, healing, rainbow water glowing with a golden hue coming from above. My near-death experience (NDE) brought clarity to why this imagery held such significance for me. It dawned on me that the golden, rainbow light I envision is actually the essence that emanates from everything on the Other Side. The energy of God. Knowing this has been incredibly helpful. Now, when I imagine this radiant light during my healing practices, it connects me to that powerful energy from beyond. It's truly a gift to access and utilize this amazing energy while we are in human form.

I visualize this light coming into the top of my head, then moving down my body, through my shoulders, down through my fingertips, back around my chest, through the trunk of my body and my pelvis, down my legs to the end of my toes, and out of my body to be absorbed back into the ground.

Next, I visualize that beautiful glowing light going through my client's body too. I set the intention for it to go through their body in a similar way, circulating up and down until it is released out through their feet where it is let go and transmuted by the Other Side. As healers, we don't always have to explain this entire process to people. Our responsibility is only to set our intention and visualize how we'd like the energy to flow. Once that step is complete, you can continue with any healing techniques or methods you usually use.

As you practice this work, I always recommend making sure that you are continually practicing boundaries and cleansing your own energy. As healers, we are called to serve and support others on their journey. We give of ourselves freely, pouring out our energy and compassion to help those in need. But in doing so, we may unknowingly take on the energy of our clients, leaving us feeling drained, depleted, and even unwell.

You don't need to self-sacrifice to be able to honor your calling as a healer or spiritual person. That's why I want to encourage you to practice the cleanse and protect ritual at the beginning of this chapter on a regular basis. It will help keep you grounded and prevent you from picking up and carrying around negative energies that don't belong to you. If you want even more protection, you can visualize a shield around your entire body any time you go out or interact with other human beings. It's helpful to visualize an energetic shield that is transparent and malleable. Creating a shield made of bricks or concrete may feel safe, but it blocks everything out. Using something you can see through keeps the bad stuff out, but still lets the light in. And more light is always a good thing.

When we create energetic boundaries and shields, we are able to protect our energy from outside influences. We can learn to recognize when we're taking on the energy of others and take steps to release it, so it doesn't negatively affect our own well-being. By protecting our own energy, we are better equipped to hold space for others and support them in their healing journey. We can approach each session with renewed energy, focus, and compassion.

So, continue this sacred work. And remember, creating energetic boundaries and a shield isn't about closing yourself off or shutting out the world. It's about protecting your energy field so you can better serve others and contribute something positive to the collective.

Chapter 9

Tapping into Your Intuition

Remember

Your soul remembers the infinite gifts you were born with.

The home we come from never truly leaves us.

*We may feel alone here on this Earth, struggling
to connect to something tangible.*

*You must look to yourself to begin to discover the energetic
connection was never fully severed when you came into this life.*

Look inward for guidance, you are capable.

Call on your guides, your higher self, and Source.

Your gifts, long buried by human doubt, can be unearthed.

Your potential is limitless, you are stronger than you know.

*Lovingly begin to recognize your purpose
is ever growing and changing.*

You only need to remember.

HAVE YOU EVER had a feeling deep in your gut, a knowingness that something is right or wrong, even if you can't quite put your finger on why? That is your intuition speaking to you. And let me tell you, connecting with your intuition can be a truly beautiful experience. What I'd like to share here is a simple step-by-step guide to how I tap into my own intuition. This is written in my own words, but also incorporates helpful advice from my spirit guides, Gayle and Jessica.

Intuitive glimpses happen all the time, even if you're not focusing on them. In your daily life, you may come across signs, hints, or cues that speak to you without having to go through the process I'm about to describe. While it's helpful to understand the steps, once you are well versed on how to connect with your intuition, it can happen naturally without you having to concentrate on it all of the time. You'll get little suggestions from your higher self or guides without even knowing it's happening. This might show up as an urge to call someone you've been thinking about, not knowing that they've been struggling. Or taking a different route to work, narrowly missing a car accident. Just because you know how to connect with your intuition doesn't mean you have to intentionally focus on it to receive guidance. It just happens.

Intuition is a powerful tool that can guide you through life's twists and turns, helping you to make decisions that align with your truest self. When you learn to connect with your intuition, you open yourself up to a world of possibilities and a deeper understanding of yourself and the world around you. But how do you connect with it? It starts with learning to listen. Our intuition speaks to us in many ways—through our emotions, our physical sensations, and even through our dreams. It's up to us to be present and aware enough to recognize these signals and trust our own inner voice.

When I want to connect with my intuition, I begin by finding a peaceful, quiet space where I can be alone. I sit with my legs uncrossed, and with both of my feet planted firmly on the ground. I visualize that I'm a tree and my feet are like the roots reaching far inside the Earth, keeping me grounded and safe. I have my hands facing palms up, with a selenite crystal in my left hand. If you don't have the ability to sit, or don't have a selenite crystal, that's okay. This is a practice that can be modified so it makes sense for you and your situation. The most important thing is that you take time to intentionally calm your mind and relax your body before you begin.

Next, I do the 4-7-8 breathing I shared with you earlier to help cleanse and protect my energy and my space. Breathe in for four seconds, hold your breath for a count of seven, and breathe out for a count of eight (or until you release all the air from your lungs.) And repeat. Do this three or four times, ensuring that you get yourself well-oxygenated and composed.

As you breathe, pay attention to your body when you do this practice. Are your breaths short and shallow? Is your body tense or anxious? Where are you holding the most stress? Honor what you feel, and allow yourself to accept whatever comes up.

This step might sound simple at first, but I think the value of deep breathing is underrated. So many of us struggle to quiet the mind, and find ourselves getting caught up in an endless stream of thoughts. And that's okay. We don't have to be perfect. We just have to get started.

While I do this, I also enjoy stretching my body and moving my arms and neck from side to side. Stretching can help release tension, and I find it helps me relax even more. Next, I recite the cleanse and protect prayer:

Please cleanse me of anything not serving a positive purpose and protect me from picking up and carrying with me anything that will not serve me well.

After you are properly cleansed and protected, that is when we can call on our spirit guides, the universe, or God. To do this, I have a poem that I read to myself; you can say it out loud if you'd like.

"Supreme Being, all that is, thank you for the opportunity to complete this [Insert whatever makes sense for you here. It could be a spiritual reading, healing, meditation, or something else]. May it be guided by your love and light. Surround me with your golden divine energy. Only the most pure, positive, highest essence is allowed in this space. Teachers, angels, spirit guides, loved ones, and guiding energies, thank you all for coming. I intend for accurate, open, clear lines of communication, amen.

Next, I like to make my own tailored requests that are related to whatever circumstances are going on at the time. For instance, if I have someone coming in to see me for an intuitive reading that day, I'll ask for insight and information to help me provide the best experience. My guides will often let me know why that person chose to come to me and offer background information about what's going on for them. If you're not doing an intuitive reading, you could ask for guidance about your situation or request a sign from the universe to help guide you in the right direction.

Keep in mind that this isn't meant to be a time to rattle off a wish list or create a mountain of requests for your spirit guides to fulfill. That's not what connecting with our intuition is meant to be about. It's more valuable to focus on gratitude for everything you have, grounded in the faith that you will be taken care of and provided for, no matter what.

If you're struggling and in search of guidance, you can explore that. It's all about how you ask. So let's say you're struggling with your career and wondering whether you should change jobs. Saying something like, "I want to know, yes or no, should I quit my job?" probably won't get you the best results. Your guides will likely be hesitant to influence you because they don't want to alter your soul's life plan. They know that even if they did answer you with "yes" or "no", it might end up causing unintended consequences.

Here's a good example of how that might play out: let's say you decide to apply for a new job and you get an interview booked on the calendar for next week. You're excited, but really nervous about how things will go, so you decide to connect with your intuition. After you cleanse and protect, you ask your guides, "Am I going to get the job?" And let's say your guides answer with a positive, "yes." After hearing that, you assume everything is going to go your way so you stop worrying about it. You throw out all the pre-interview preparation you normally would have done and show up completely unprepared. After everything is said and done, you don't get a job offer after all.

A scenario like this doesn't mean your guides were wrong; they just had a different perspective. When you originally asked them for guidance about your future, they saw a timeline where you did prepare, where you did plan, and where you walked into that interview having done the work. But because you chose to do things differently, everything shifted. That's why guides are hesitant to answer yes or no questions or provide concrete responses. What they say or do can take you off course, and that's the last thing they want to have happen.

For other situations, though, they may feel like giving you an answer can have a positive effect. A good example could be something like this: let's say you've struggled with saying "no" your whole life. You always want to help people and feel guilty turning down requests. Then one day, you find yourself in a situation where you finally set some really good boundaries at work or maybe with someone in your family. It was super hard to do, but you stood up for yourself. Afterward, maybe you're feeling a little uneasy about it, so you decide to check in with your guides to see if you did the right thing. Usually, with a scenario like this, you will get an answer from your spirit guides, and the answer will come to you the moment you ask.

The guidance you receive may sound like your own voice, or it might come through as a gut feeling, a sudden insight, or a series of synchronicities. Other times, their message may be more subtle, like a gentle nudge or a feeling of peace. No matter what, the first response you get is usually the accurate one.

When I connect intuitively it feels like a very light vibration, like butterflies fluttering in my chest. Sometimes it will be ringing in the ears, and occasionally will feel like my whole body is buzzing. What does it feel like for you? Have you begun to discover what connecting intuitively feels like in your body? Is it butterflies? Are your ears ringing too? Do you ever see things pass by in your peripheral vision? All of these are signs.

What If I Don't Get a Response?

Another part of connecting intuitively is learning how to determine when a non-answer from your guides is the answer. So, for example, if you have sat down twenty times to ask about something going on in your life and you haven't received an answer at all, that's probably the answer. Situations like this may leave you feeling anxious, uncertain, or indecisive, but your guides aren't answering you for a reason. They recognize you are struggling with a very human moment, but want to honor that this is something your soul chose to go through. They know, from a higher energetic perspective, that you are fully capable of handling what you're going through without their known, palpable, tangible support. This doesn't mean they have disappeared. Instead, they are allowing you to learn the lessons life has to offer. They are not always going to make it easier for us. That's not their job. Their job is to walk with us and hold us up when we can't hold ourselves up.

Is it Intuition or Your Own Mind?

As you practice tapping into your intuition, you might be curious about how to distinguish between your intuition and your mind or ego. Your intuition manifests as a strong, intuitive knowing or a "gut feeling" in your core. It's a sense of inner certainty that doesn't rely on logical reasoning. The guidance you get from your intuition feels clear and will resonate with your deepest self. It often comes on spontaneously and unexpectedly, like a flash of insight or a new perspective that emerges seemingly out of nowhere.

Thoughts and feelings can be loud, overwhelming, and based in fear. When your mind interferes, it might sound like, "But, what if I really did hurt their feelings when I set that boundary?" "What if they never talk to me again?" "What if I started something really bad?" "What if they hate me now?" Our minds are often functioning from a place of ego with the intention of protecting us from perceived threats. This doesn't mean our mind or ego is bad; it just means that it isn't the same thing as our intuition.

If you're tapping into your intuitive gifts, and you feel you're connecting with something negative or low-vibe, it's a signal that something is off-balance or there is some sort of interference. A lot of the time when this happens, we are unconsciously connecting with the energies of people we know. We're allowing their energy into our space, and it's affecting us in a way that doesn't feel good. It's important to pay attention to these intuitive clues as they can guide us to make choices that promote our well-being and protect our energetic boundaries.

Before I accepted my gifts, I worked at a medical detox as a rehabilitation worker. I remember talking with different people and I would always just instinctively know what to say. They might say something or ask a question, then all of a sudden I'd start to respond and it would feel like my whole body was vibrating from the inside out. Words would just flow out of me without me even thinking about it, and I would tell them exactly what they needed to hear. At the end of our conversation, people would often look at me and say, "Oh my gosh. Thank you so much! You always know what to say." The other person would walk away feeling great, but I almost always felt a little anxious afterward and had trouble sleeping at night.

At the time, I didn't know that I was connecting with

my guides; I just understood that I would always know what advice to give even though I didn't know how. Looking back now, I realize I wasn't setting good boundaries. I wasn't cleansing and protecting. I was letting any and all energy into my body, which left me feeling exhausted all the time. Experiences like this are good reminders about how crucial it is to establish healthy boundaries in everyday life. Trust your intuition and tune into how you feel. If you're experiencing feelings of discomfort or unease, pay attention to that. It's okay to take care of yourself, just like how you take care of other people.

Deepening the Connection with Your Guides

If you're interested in deepening your connection with your guides, you can start by gently concentrating and asking them to come forward. You may not sense anything right away, and that's nothing to worry about. Sometimes it takes a long time before they make themselves known. Other times, they won't come forward because, for one reason or another, they don't feel it's in your best interest. It's important that we don't become obsessive in this process of trying to sense them, but rather open to whatever might happen. If you are someone who is genuinely curious about getting to know them so you have a better visual or understanding of your guides, they will likely show themselves eventually. Even if they don't, you can always go to a trusted psychic or someone like me to get a clearer picture of who they are.

Keep in mind that connecting intuitively does not mean that you always have to focus on your guides. You might not know who they are or what they look like. I know it took me many months to get to know all of my spirit guides and recognize the signs. Over time, I learned that they will often make their presence known to me with things like repeating numbers, a meaningful song, pennies, feathers, hummingbirds, or ladybugs. For you, the signs might be different. In my experience, it's unique to each person and it's something that happens naturally and organically without us even trying. You don't have to worry about establishing a connection because it's already there.

Instead, you can simply focus on tuning into your higher self, the universe, Mother Earth, a loved one who passed, or anything that resonates with you. There are many beings on the Other Side who are there to support and love us. They won't always tell you what to do or where to go, but they will stand with you in support of your human experience.

As we continue on our spiritual journey and begin to learn how to follow our intuition and listen to our guides, we may be led down paths or directions we didn't anticipate or plan for. This can feel surprising or uncomfortable, especially when we have an idea in our mind of how things should be. However, it's important to fully understand that we plan this human life and know exactly what we should do at any given moment. Even if our human self feels lost, our soul never is.

Because our guides are on the Other Side, they're able to look at the life plan our soul made and can anticipate opportunities for learning and growth. These learning opportunities may not always seem great from our human perspective, but on the Other Side nothing is good or bad. Everything we walk through in life is seen as an incredible opportunity to evolve and become more enlightened.

Using the job analogy again, let's say you're on the fence about changing jobs and you ask your guides if you should apply at a different company. They respond with an affirmative "yes." So, you apply for the new position and get the job. But after a few months, you realize that you're working for a horrible, narcissist boss who is a complete nightmare. You feel like you have to assert yourself all the time, you have to set new boundaries constantly, and you're not enjoying it at all. In a scenario like that, you might think to yourself, "What the heck, guides? I asked you guys if I should change jobs, and now I'm living in hell every day." But what you might not see is the enormous amount of growth you're experiencing, not just as a person but as a soul. On the Other Side, difficulty is one of the greatest paths to enlightenment. It's not seen as a "bad" experience. It's something to be embraced.

No matter what happens, trust that you are enough exactly as you are. You are never on the wrong path or going in the wrong direction. Life is all about learning. Full stop. And during the times when you're really suffering, when you feel anxious, angry, or hurt, and you don't know what to do or what to say, your guides are right there with you. They are always closer than you think, offering you unconditional love and support.

My guides have walked with me down many difficult paths, and there are a couple of things I do when I'm at the end of my rope. Sometimes I'll talk to my guides to let them know I'm not in a place to take on any more hard things for a while. It's not something I do all the time because I understand that, as a human, I'm meant to walk through these lessons. But occasionally, I think we all need a break and asking for one is okay.

Other times, when things get really hard, I connect with them using gratitude meditation. When you first hear about gratitude meditation, it might sound a little odd. I mean, when we're suffering and going through really shitty stuff, we don't always feel like offering gratitude. But it has surprising benefits. I'm not talking about toxic positivity here. I'm talking about focusing on gratitude for life while embracing the support and reassurance from your guides, who are constantly there to remind you that you are never walking alone. Because when we cultivate gratitude, we shift our focus from what is lacking to what we already have. This shift in perspective can be incredibly powerful and can help us find hope, joy, and meaning even in the darkest of times.

I personally find gratitude meditations especially helpful when I'm struggling with patience. It's one of my life lessons, and it's something that's always been really hard for me. On the days where I feel like I could really use support with it, I start with a cleanse and protect prayer, close my eyes, then say something like, "Spirit guides, thank you for always walking with me, even when it's hard. I'm just asking today that you really do come forward and help me with patience. I know, and I have faith, that I'm able to be more patient than what I am right now. I know I am learning from my lack of patience, but I just ask today that you step forward and help me with forgiveness of myself because today I am truly struggling with how my impatience affects myself and the people in my life." Almost without fail, I can feel my guides come through and it makes all the difference in the world.

My wish for you when you are hurting, as so many of us are, is that even if you aren't connecting with your guides you find hope knowing that there is a higher power that is looking out for you. We aren't meant to suffer every day. That's not our purpose. Human life is cherished on the Other Side, and they want to see us thrive, even in the face of great difficulty. So when it feels right, take the time to cleanse and protect, have gratitude, and ask for what you need at any given moment. And rest assured that without a doubt, your guides are with you 100% of the time, even if you never notice them.

Chapter 10

The Power of Empaths

I Am an Empath

You're too sensitive, they say.

Toughen up or you'll never survive.

Why can't they see that I'm feeling for you too?

When you hurt, I carry it with me.

When you are frightened, I am scared too.

I take it into my soul and it waits for a way to purge itself.

I close my eyes and see the pain of the world.

I wake up with a feeling of dread.

I know in my soul it doesn't belong to me, yet I struggle to let it go.

*When the joy comes, I wait with bated
breath for it to be stripped away.*

I know it is fleeting and will be overshadowed by heaviness.

I feel the world in every waking moment.

I work endlessly to cleanse my human body, refresh my soul.

You're too sensitive, they say.

I have to be, so you can breathe.

IN A WORLD that often feels cold and unfeeling, empaths stand out as beacons of compassion and understanding. These sensitive souls have the ability to sense and absorb the emotions of those around them, often to the point of feeling overwhelmed by the intensity of the feelings they pick up on.

At its core, empathy is the ability to understand and share the feelings of another person. While most of us are capable of empathy to some degree, empaths take this ability to a whole new level. They have an innate sensitivity to the emotions of others, and are able to pick up on even the most subtle of cues.

It is not uncommon for empaths to feel like they don't fit in, as their unique sensitivity and heightened awareness of energy can create a sense of being different from those around them. These are the people who often hear things like, "Why are you so sensitive?" "Why are you taking that so personally?" "Why does that bother you? It doesn't even affect you." "What do you mean you can't watch the news or certain movies?" "Why do you care so much about those people? You don't even know them." I know this was the case with me. My whole life, I didn't understand what was wrong with me. I might have even called myself overly dramatic. But in reality, nothing was wrong with me. I was just an empath picking up other people's energy and not realizing I was doing it.

Another sign that someone is an empath is their undeniable connection with animals. Pets identify with empathic energy because pets are empathic themselves. I remember how my dog used to come up to me for everything. No matter how many other people were around, he'd walk up to me and just stare at me. He would never do this to anyone else, but he did it to me all the time. He knew he could come to me because I'd understand what he wanted. So if he was hungry or thirsty, I would remind the kids to refill his water, or I'd get up and get him some food. It's the kind of non-verbal communication that empaths exchange with animals without even thinking about it.

As empaths, we have a similar energetic exchange with the people in our lives too. We experience connections and relationships so much deeper than surface level. We can see behind the smile. We can relate to you genuinely and authentically, making you feel seen and heard. For me personally, this means I can see the world differently than a lot of people because I can literally see feelings. I can see where you're coming from, how you got there, and where you're going. I can read your soul and see all of your lives. I can see if you're crying because you're sad or if you're crying because you're feeling guilt or shame. I can see if you're smiling on the outside but miserable on the inside.

Maybe you've experienced something similar. Maybe you have a heightened sensitivity to the emotions, thoughts, and energies of others. This ability to easily pick up on the moods and vibrations in the environment is an incredible gift, but it's a gift that we have to protect. As empaths, we take on all this energy, and it affects us not just emotionally but physically as well. An empath will actually feel that other person's sadness. They will feel their anger, their joy. An empath absorbs any emotion another person might be feeling and takes it on as their own. They can quite literally look at another human and physically feel what they're feeling. When this happens, the empath is often deeply affected by the other person, whether they know them or not.

Over time, as the empath picks up all this stuff from other people, it can feel overwhelming. I like to think of it like this:

Picture all the humans on Earth. You're there too, and you are carrying the perfect size suitcase that is decorated just the way you like it. It's not too big, and it's not too small. It's just perfect for you to carry around. As you walk through life, once in a while, your suitcase starts to feel a little light, so you add some stuff. Sometimes your suitcase starts to feel a little heavy, so you let a few things go. But it's always balanced. Empathic people are carrying around the same kind of suitcase, but as they're walking around, they approach people and say, "Your suitcase looks too heavy. Let me take some of that weight off for you. It'll help make it easier." They continue this with every person they come across. So they travel through life, making everyone else's life better, but they go home at the end of the day dragging fifteen suitcases behind them, feeling completely drained and exhausted. Even if nothing bad happens to piss them off, they carry around this heavy energy, and over time, it gets to be a lot.

If the empath doesn't find a way to release all the built-up energy and burdens they've picked up, it will come out in other ways. Sometimes, this will show up as an empath picking a fight with someone we love because we're unconsciously trying to find an outlet. Other times, empaths can grow resentful, like their needs are never met, and feel like they do everything for everyone else and don't get anything in return. God knows I used to be like this. I used to pick fights with my husband and get really upset, but I try not to do that anymore. Now if I start feeling that way, I'll walk, I'll read a book, I'll take a bath, or I'll find quiet time for myself to sit in meditation as I visualize the weight coming off as I set down all those suitcases. It's not always easy, but being aware of the emotions you need to release can help.

What makes it even more tricky is that empaths are natural chameleons. We can adapt to just about any situation or any group. If we are around a lot of loud people, we'll become quieter so they can speak. If we are around quieter people, we'll get a little bit louder to bring others out of their shells. If we are desperate for a connection, we'll slowly change ourselves to become exactly what the other person needs, even if that other person or people didn't suit us in the first place.

This dynamic shows up a lot in relationships with friends and the people we love. So, if someone calls an empath and says, "Hey, I want to get together, I'd love to get your advice. Let's grab a coffee." The empath will agree to go. And when they meetup, the friend starts telling the empath what's going on in their life and explains the problem they are dealing with. The empath listens carefully, and when it's time to respond, they say exactly what their friend needs to hear with genuine compassion and understanding. Their friend's mouth drops open, and they say, "Oh my gosh! I never thought of it that way. That makes so much sense. Thank you!" The two friends say goodbye, and the friend goes home feeling absolutely amazing and energized. The empath, on the other hand, leaves feeling completely exhausted and desperate for a nap. It happens like this because the empath absorbs the negative energies from the other person, often without realizing it. This exposure to a wide spectrum of emotions can lead to energetic overload, which can be mentally, emotionally, and physically draining.

Empaths have huge hearts and experience the world in such a beautiful way. When someone is going through a hard time, our impulse is to go above and beyond to make sure everyone around us is happy. We like to help people because we don't like seeing anyone or anything hurting or suffering. It's our natural instinct to try to help and take that pain away. But sometimes, we can get caught up in this so much that we do it at our own detriment. Because of this dynamic, I truly believe needy energies are drawn to empathic people simply because we can give them what they want. It creates a scenario where the empath often feels taken advantage of, like they do everything for everyone else and get little to nothing in return.

This can show up in relationships where the empath feels like the other person keeps taking and taking until one day, the empath gets fed up and says, "I'm done. You always take advantage of me. You don't see me. Everything is always about you." But what empaths don't realize is all the stuff you've been feeling inside was never obvious to the other person. Many people can't read energy or bring in the same level of energetic sensitivity as empaths. When I say that, please know that it's not a judgment. It's just the way it is.

I think this is important to keep in mind because empaths don't have the luxury of only interacting with other empaths. They have to interact with the full spectrum of human beings, from the people who are highly sensitive to the humans who aren't sensitive at all. As empaths, we can't expect non-empathic people to read our energy. Not everyone can do what we do. Not everyone has the capability to be more sensitive. We have to use our words to communicate how we're feeling and ask for what we need.

In the process, it is our job to protect ourselves. If empaths continue giving their energy unconditionally without setting boundaries, cleansing their energy, or saying "no," they are going to attract needy, selfish, narcissistic people. It might be hard to hear, but it's an unfortunate truth. If we as empaths are willing to have a completely unbalanced relationship (as opposed to a mutually beneficial relationship where two people are working toward shared happiness), it won't feel good.

Unchecked empathy without boundaries can manifest as sickness, both mentally and physically. When your mind, body, and spirit connection is off, everything is off. This can look like depression and anxiety, circulation problems, endometriosis, iron deficiency, digestive issues, and more. Empaths also tend to have issues with their thyroid and adrenals. It's not uncommon for very strong empaths to carry excess weight around their bellies as well. It's the body's way of adding an extra layer of protection so you don't absorb too much energy.

This doesn't mean empaths are destined for a life of health problems or unbalanced relationships. We can take our power back by shifting our focus and ending cycles of over-giving. By doing this, we gain back control of when and if we engage or absorb the energy around us. I've had to do this in my own life, and while it isn't easy, I can honestly say it's made all the difference. Before the stroke, I was leading a life filled with happiness, joy, and balance. Now, I'm working on achieving that same level of balance while adapting to my new circumstances. I firmly believe that achieving harmony and balance in life is 100% possible for everyone.

One thing that has helped me is remembering that, yes, we are spiritual beings made of energy, but we are also human. There is a very real separation between who we are as souls and how our lives are playing out here on Earth. When I had my NDE, I saw this firsthand. On the Other Side, there is only love and unconditional support. But here, there is everything else—hatred, jealousy, anger, pain, suffering, betrayal, trauma, and more. That is why boundaries are so vital. Our physical bodies do not work the same way as our spiritual bodies do on the Other Side. It's our job, especially as empaths, to protect ourselves.

Chapter 11

Setting Boundaries

Power

She woke, even as she breathed, she could feel her power.
In the sky, she could glimpse her limitless potential.
In the Earth, she recognized the depths to which her soul could grow.
Tree roots mirrored the connection she could feel to all living things.
Every breath a new beginning, infinite opportunity.
She rose from the cradle of mother nature.
Stood tall and strong, letting the grass give energy to her bare feet.
In this she felt comforted, knowing she was loved.
A human in its nature appears ever taking.
Stripping this planet of its resources, baring her soul for all to see.
One person can make a difference, breathing
life back into the lifeless.
As she stands, she envisions all things connected.
She feels the energy of all she touches, sees, smells.
All is not lost, we are not beyond repair.
One soul embracing the way it should be.
Seeing the infinite glory, we are gifted at birth.
Take a moment to raise yourself up.
Celebrate your innate humanness.
Stand, bare feet to soil, soul to all that is.
Let go of the limits which have bound you so tight.
You are beautiful, connected, celebrated, and whole.
The sky is your limit, the Earth is your depth.
Fully awaken, breathe and own your power.

SETTING BOUNDARIES IS an empowering practice that allows you to honor your needs, preserve your energy, and maintain healthy relationships. You can start by cultivating self-awareness and understanding your own needs, values, and limits. Reflect on what is important to you and what feels comfortable or uncomfortable in various situations. This awareness will serve as a foundation for establishing boundaries that align with your authentic self.

It helps to identify the specific boundaries you want to set. Be clear about what you will and will not tolerate in terms of behavior, time commitments, emotional availability, or personal space. Clearly defining what you're okay or not okay with will make it easier to communicate with others. Learning to recognize and identify what you want or need takes time and patience, so be gentle with yourself as you walk through this process.

When you do communicate, don't be afraid to do so assertively. In my personal life, I tend to be very blunt, which is hard for some people. But I've found that being blunt at the moment is much better than not being honest about how I feel. If I avoid saying something or suppress what I'm really feeling, I know I will take it with me, and that negative energy will just fester. So, if someone is mad at me or says something insensitive, I'll respond with something like, "Hey, it feels like you're angry with me or something is going on. Do we need to have a conversation about that?" Or, "Hey, the energy I'm getting from this is X. Let me know if I'm wrong or if this is totally way off. Let's talk about it." Not everyone likes that. We live in a society where we avoid confrontation and try to be pleasant. I don't live in that world anymore. It's too hard for me.

But communication as an empath doesn't have to be blunt. You can find a way to talk to people that feels right for you. In my experience, it's all about learning to express ourselves without anger. A big part of that is taking a pause before you react. When you're trying to set boundaries and you get triggered, it's only human to feel upset and have thoughts like, "Why are they so difficult? Why can't they see?! It's so frustrating and makes me so mad!" Try not to let that anger consume you. Remember, you may not be able to control the things that happen around you, but you can always control your response. So when you can, wait before you react. Take a few deep breaths. Scream into a pillow. Do some physical exercise. Those are all great ways to release that energy.

As you begin your boundary setting journey, be prepared for a little grief. If you've gone through life as an empath with flexible or no boundaries, needy people have likely taken advantage of you. Most of the time, one or both of you didn't realize this was happening. However, when you begin altering the energy you contribute in the relationship, there will be pushback. As soon as you're no longer willing to self-sacrifice and begin setting boundaries and verbalizing those boundaries, people who have benefited from your over-giving won't like it. In my own life, I found that once I wasn't okay with doing energetic counseling constantly or fixing everything for everyone, certain relationships no longer served their purpose. I'd learned what I needed from them, they'd learned what they needed from me, and we parted ways.

The other thing that can happen is that your romantic relationship may shift and change (I speak from experience.) I met my husband when he was a very young twenty-one-year-old, and I was a very emotionally mature twenty-three-year-old.

He was still living at home and being taken care of, and at the time I was ready and willing to take care of anything and everyone that fell into my path. Very quickly, he became one more person I was taking care of. In a way, it felt like I replaced his mother, rather than becoming an equal partner in the relationship. When I accepted my gifts and began learning how to distinguish between my need to nurture myself and my tendency to look after others, I was no longer willing to give away my energy.

We both knew things had to change or our relationship wouldn't work anymore. Over time, I learned to be more verbal about my needs and got better at communication overall. My husband learned a lot too. He started to understand that I wanted different things, and sometimes, that meant I needed more time alone, especially when I was overwhelmed. He also started to respond differently when I insisted on taking care of everything. This became abundantly clear when I had the stroke, as it marked the first time in our relationship when he had to take care of everything. He truly rose to the occasion and rocked it. And over time, our relationship has changed, but it changed for the better. I think in any relationship we have in life, we have to determine for ourselves how much time and effort we're willing to put in. We have to decide if it's worth it to continue.

If you have people in your life you know you should walk away from due to an energy imbalance, try to have gratitude for this process. Even if they treated you horribly the entire time you knew them, be grateful because, in a strange way, they helped you grow. You wouldn't be the person you are today if you hadn't been around that really difficult energy who never saw your needs. When you think back on your time with them, try not to fall into the trap of thinking, "Oh, they were such an asshole. They never cared about me." Maybe it's not that they never cared. Maybe they weren't capable of caring the same way you are. Maybe they aren't empathic and will never be able to feel things the way you do. Maybe, just maybe, they were put into your life solely to help you establish these boundaries. It's okay for you to create separation from that person. When you do, you might just notice how many other people are attracted to your newfound energy, which is beautiful because it's balanced, reciprocal, and feels wonderful.

Just don't forget to take good care of yourself. Engage in self-care practices which nurture your well-being and reinforce your boundaries. Prioritize activities that bring you joy, relaxation, and rejuvenation. Taking care of yourself helps maintain your boundaries and reinforces your commitment to self-respect. You can do this in a few different ways. For instance, you could try dedicating a physical space in your home where you can retreat and recharge. Fill it with comforting and calming elements, like soft lighting, cozy blankets, or soothing music. Carve out regular moments of solitude in your day-to-day life to reflect, recharge, and be present with your own thoughts and emotions. Spend time in nature to restore your energy; it has a soothing and grounding effect on empaths. When you do go out, try visualizing a protective shield of light around you, affirming that only positive and nourishing energies can enter your space.

Something that has really helped me, both with self-care and boundaries overall, is incorporating the cleanse and protect prayer into my daily life. I know I have already talked about it, but it's worth repeating.

Please cleanse me of anything not serving a positive
purpose and protect me from picking up and carrying
with me anything that will not serve me well.

When I first accepted my spiritual gifts, I'd say the cleanse and protect prayer fifty to sixty times a day. I made it a habit to repeat it whenever I walked through a doorway. I'd also say the prayer a few hours ahead of time if I knew I would have to spend time around people who affected my energy in a not-so-great way. It's something I started doing all the time without thinking about it. After about six months, my spirit guides and higher self caught on and said, "Oh, okay. Every time she takes her kids to school or is in this situation over here, she wants to be protected and doesn't want to feel anything from anybody." And it worked. Things got easier, and I stopped feeling so overwhelmed by the people and circumstances around me.

Over the years, I've continued using the cleanse and protect prayer, and it's never let me down. Because I've said it so many times, it's become a natural part of who I am and the boundaries are always there. Although I don't feel the need to say it fifty times a day anymore, I still use it before I do any spiritual work or when I'm feeling stressed out. I know I'm very affected by other people's energy, and I accept the fact that I'm going to have to protect myself continuously.

Trust me when I say that I know talking about boundaries is easier said than done. However, it can be helpful to remember that each of our souls planned out our lives before we were born. Each of us planned to walk through certain lessons, no matter how painful they might appear from our human perspective. Even if you have the best intentions, some things will never change, and they were never meant to. Empaths aren't here to save or rescue people. We are simply here to experience life in all its forms and let others do the same. That doesn't mean we can't be loving, compassionate people. It means that as empaths, we need to use discernment and be mindful about who, what, and how we engage with the world. I think it all starts with getting really comfortable saying "no."

Saying "No"

I've always been bad at saying "no," especially when I know I'm capable of helping. It took me a long time to get past the overwhelming feeling of guilt. I used to feel like I couldn't say "no" even when I wanted to. If someone wasn't sure what to do or how to do it, my heart would bleed for them until I stepped in in some way. What I've learned since accepting my gifts is that people are fully capable of figuring things out on their own. I truly believe every human on this planet knows what they need to do, and my participation (or lack thereof) doesn't affect that. Sure, I'll still say yes and help out sometimes, but I don't feel guilty anymore when I can't or don't want to do something.

For anyone who really struggles to say "no," please remember that setting boundaries and prioritizing your own well-being is an act of self-care and self-respect. Your needs, emotions, and energy are just as valid and important as anyone else's. You deserve to have boundaries and to honor them without guilt. Embrace the truth that taking care of yourself enables you to show up as your best self in all areas of your life. Treat yourself with the same compassion and understanding you extend to others. You deserve all the beautiful things life has to offer.

If someone asks you to do something, and you get a pit in your stomach and aren't sure about what to do, remember this: your emotions are important signals from your higher self about what's in alignment for you and your well-being. When you're on the fence about anything or anyone, try asking yourself questions like, "What is going to happen to me if I do this? Am I going to feel tired? Am I going to feel regretful? Shameful? Angry?" If your answer is yes to any of these things, it's a red flag. Listen to your gut. Honor your first instinct. By doing so, you'll know you're listening to your inner knowing and being honest about what you do or don't want to do.

After all, if you're saying "yes" when you really want to say "no," it will more than likely make you feel awful. It generally doesn't end well for the other person, either. For instance, if you can't stand being around someone, but you decide to take on their energy and enable them so you can tolerate them, it will take a toll on your mind, body, and soul. It also hinders the other person's journey. By stepping in and caring for them, you're helping them avoid lessons they were meant to walk through. The lesson may be put off for a time, but it will come around for them again, and the next time it may be harder. In situations like these, it's sometimes better to detach and let go, rather than try to fix it. The way I see it is, if you have people in your life who you still struggle with because all they do is continually take your energy without reciprocation, maybe they shouldn't be in your life anymore.

I recognize hearing this might not be easy. It's tough because empathic people crave to be needed. This desire fills the gaping hole inside of us that hurts for humanity, Mother Earth, and all living beings. When we focus on someone else, even briefly, it temporarily makes us feel better. However, in the process, we risk becoming somewhat addicted to the chaos. We can find ourselves trapped in a loop of putting everyone else before ourselves, neglecting our own needs and desires. Over time, this may lead to feelings of resentment, anger, sadness, anxiety, or even depression. When we reach this point, it is very easy to become suspicious of everyone and every scenario. We might even start believing that everyone is out to get us, and we may become miserable people who constantly question other people's motives. If you're at that stage, you really need to cleanse and protect and set better boundaries. Those practices can really help.

Remember, you will never be able to control everything around you, but you hold so much power. You choose what you let in and what you don't. You choose the boundaries you set. You choose your absorption level of energy. You choose how you're going to exist in the world. And how you respond makes all the difference. Take control. Let the world know, let your spirit guides know, let your higher self know that you're going to embrace being empathic, but you're not going to try to fix the world to your own detriment.

Set yourself free by setting your intention to become balanced and protected. Become an empath who has embraced their gifts but honors their limits and sets healthy boundaries. Embrace who you are as a well-rounded person who knows their worth and doesn't beat themselves up, even if it means letting other people down. It may not feel easy right away, and it's going to take a ton of practice, but I can tell you from personal experience that it's worth it.

Important Benchmarks

If you want to test how you're doing with boundaries, think of the neediest person in your life (we all have one) and invite them out to lunch. Say to yourself, "I'm going to go into this cleansed and protected, and I'm going to take little breaks during our time together to repeat the cleanse and protect prayer." Try it and see how you feel afterward. There should be a noticeable difference from the previous time that you were with them. Then the next time you plan to see this person, intentionally do not set boundaries. When you leave the get together, check in with yourself, notice how you feel, feel the energy you are carrying. I guarantee you will feel much more exhausted and anxious without the boundary setting.

You will know you're getting better with boundaries when you feel a sense of empowerment and control over your life. You'll feel like you're able to make choices that are in alignment with your needs and values. You may feel less drained because you will be protecting your energy from people and situations that take a toll on you. As a result, the quality of your relationships will improve. You will feel more seen and heard by those around you, and you'll be able to create deeper and more meaningful connections. When you are able to express your needs and have them respected by others, it's a sign that your boundaries are working and you have surrounded yourself with the right people.

Remember, setting healthy boundaries is an ongoing process, and it's okay to make mistakes and learn from them. It's okay if things don't go as planned, or if you fall back into old patterns. What matters is that you keep trying and you continue to work on learning and growing in a way that feels authentic to you. If you're struggling, don't be afraid to ask for help. We are so used to fixing everyone else, sometimes it's hard to put the focus on ourselves. It's tough to ask for help when you're used to being the helper. But it can make things so much better; I know it has for me. I have people I call when I'm really going through it. Find someone you feel you can talk to, and please know you are never alone.

Chapter 12

Channeled Messages from the Other Side

A channeled message from my spirit guide, Peter: Freedom is a concept. We are enough.

It is so strange to me to see a place which is supposed to be the land of the free; when freedom does not really exist here.

Freedom is a concept, something that blows by in the wind. People who live in these western countries do not realize we are controlled by the media, controlled by what we see every day. We are controlled by electronics and frequencies that exist to tell us what to do, how to live, and what is acceptable.

In a world where we feel free, where we feel we can speak our minds and do what we want, when we want, we are not realizing by following the norm, by conforming to society, by allowing outside influences to tell us how to live our lives, what is right, how to think, how to feel, choose a side, up and down, black and white, you can only believe one way, and every other way is wrong or you can't be that one thing, you have to be something else, we are not free.

There is always something telling us what to do, how to live, where to go, up and down, black and white and living like that is not free.

Freedom is waking up in the morning and not judging, not feeling like you are less than or more than because of where you live or what you look like, the color of your skin, or what your body possesses.

Freedom is being able to say what you want when you want, live peacefully and with love and not feel you are being judged for that. Places on this planet, which claim they are the land of the free because I can own what I want and do what I want with the things I possess, are not free. You are creating a prison for yourself to live in while other people live in similar prisons.

Your belief system creates your surroundings, creates your reality, and creates the people who exist with you.

If you are looking at other people and judging them for not believing what you believe, or not looking through the same lens as you, you are not free.

More than 65% of humans on this earth wake up every morning feeling like a failure. We dwell on the fact we do not have enough time, not enough energy, not enough of a voice; we believe we are not good enough, tall enough, beautiful enough, rich enough, smart enough, busy enough, chill enough, or not enlightened enough. There will come a day where we can wake up and know we are enough just by existing.

We are human. We are here, we are surviving, we are doing what we need to do, and that is enough. Until people can realize that, there will be this fight, this battle, this fight to the death of who is better than/more than/less than. A hierarchy of humanness, a ranking system for success, but who sets that system if not people who know nothing about us, know nothing about each individual? Society tells us we are failing, but if you wake up each day you are fulfilling your purpose, you are not failing; you are successful. If you wake up happy in the morning, joyful, centered, grounded, and knowing that your existence here has a purpose. That is success! That is freedom!

WHAT YOU'LL READ next are channeled messages from my spirit guide Peter. They are here to provide insight into all of your "big picture" questions about the universe, the state of humanity, and more. I hope you enjoy them.

How is a soul formed?

A soul is energy and on the Other Side energy begets energy. All souls are created by that highest energy and all souls return to it. Time and space do not exist, so there is no meter for a soul's life. Amber explains it well with her raincloud description. Envision your soul as a raincloud and all your lives are raindrops coming from the cloud. They are formed, travel into a life, live the life, and then are reabsorbed back into the rain cloud. The highest energy is the first and biggest rain cloud and every other rain cloud is created by it.

What is it like on the Other Side? Is there a hierarchy of souls?

No, there is no hierarchy or monarchy. On the Other Side there is only love; no one soul is better or worse than another. There is no judgment. In saying that, there is a range of energies and each energy carries its own frequency. The highest energy many people call God. You can call it whatever feels right for you. God does not have a gender or a human form. It is an overwhelming energy of love that you can not ignore when in its presence. God energy is a part of the grass, the flowers, the trees, the other souls—everything. It is more beautiful than anything you have seen in this human world.

The next level of energy are angels. Angels have not lived a physical life. They are higher dimensional beings who stay on the Other Side to check in and help humans on Earth stay on track. They make sure the things that are meant to happen do, and the things that aren't meant to happen don't. Even though angels are not human beings, they can take human form. Many people have heard stories of people who have a brush with death, only to be saved at the last minute by an unknown person. A common one is the story about someone who gets into a car wreck in the middle of nowhere, and they are panicking because their car is about to catch on fire. Then all of a sudden, a stranger shows up to help them and pulls them free from the car and saves their life. Eventually, the police come and ask, "How did you get out of that car when you did?" And the person answers, "Oh, well, there was this guy who came and pulled me out but I don't know where they went." That would be an example of an encounter with an angel.

Angels come and do things like that all the time. Same idea if a person is on the verge of dying, but the Other Side knows they must live, angels will come and comfort them until they can get help. Or, if some decision or event is going to really affect the collective consciousness as a whole, they'll come in. You might not think that one person's decision makes that big of a difference, but it does. Let's say somebody is being abused and needs help to get out of that situation. Maybe they've been kidnapped and are trapped in a dark basement with no way out. Angels might intervene because the kidnapped person is supposed to be a pivotal activist for effecting change, particularly for women who have been abused or abducted. Maybe this one person is meant to really help the world. Angels will come in to help. That is part of their role on the Other Side.

Do angels pay attention to our day-to-day lives?

A human way to view angels is that they, like me, are concerned with the collective enlightenment and growth of the world. They will manifest themselves in human form if it means changing or stopping something which may affect the enlightenment of the collective consciousness in a way that is not beneficial for humankind. When needed, angels are capable of creating the Mandela effect—a phenomenon that refers to a collective timeline shift that changes history, often to prevent disaster or man-made destruction.

Do angels watch over certain things or people?

Yes, there are angels and guides for specific things and tasked with watching over caregivers, or other segments of humanity. Angels can have certain passions, and can choose to focus solely on those passions when doing their work. Essentially it is completely up to each angel when and where they interact with humans and our planet.

How many souls are there?

There are millions of souls and billions of humans on the planet at this moment. That's not counting all the other souls in other dimensions. This fact sometimes makes some people panic a little, as it is hard to make sense of this in our brains. I promise, each life is valuable and significant. Time and space just don't exist on the Other Side, so many more things are possible.

Are we living in a matrix?

Existence here is almost like a hologram. Souls create life and live life in their created reality to learn the lessons they need to learn in order to raise their energetic vibration. And because you created your reality, who's to say that you didn't create Amber and everyone else in your life? There's nothing to say that every human created on this planet couldn't just be a creation of yours, placed in your path to help your soul do the things it needs to do in order to ascend in the spiritual realm. This is a much larger conversation, but that will have to wait for another book.

Are there numerous life forms on other planets?

Yes, life exists on Earth and in other dimensions. This includes our galaxy, other planets, other universes, and other energetic planes of existence as well as the Other Side.

At this moment on Earth, there are more frequent observations of what you call UFO's. What humans have not learned yet is that those objects and those beings are often humans from a time in the future, coming back to try to help prevent humanity from destroying itself. In this physical time, humans are not yet aware that "time" at some point will no longer be needed. In dimensions far in the future, they have mastered this manipulation of time and are now coming back in order to try to help. This is only one example of a connection between dimensions. There are also aliens in other dimensions who look much different than us, and dimensions you as humans will never see. As humans become more enlightened, access to never before seen dimensions will be opened up.

Can Peter speak to the collective consciousness now and in the future?

He shows me infinite, super old humans sitting around a table discussing what is happening with the world. They are talking about what could be changed, what we could do to go back in time and do things in a different way. They are showing a lot of interest in the entire learning process humanity is going through. The collective consciousness is ever evolving and every moment in existence helps to raise or shift it.

He says it is interesting because even now, empaths are looked at as overly sensitive people who get caught up in a lot of drama. The reality is, it would take a whole world filled with empaths to move the collective consciousness forward enough that we would stop hurting each other, and that is not going to happen for quite some time.

Are energetic portals real?

When we talk about human history, many people have beliefs or theories about where things have come from, how things were built. Take the pyramids in Egypt, for instance. Humans know they were built, but they don't fully understand how.

The people living at that time didn't have the tools to do it, but magically they were perfectly placed in this wonderful energetic setting. It is because humans didn't build them, they were created by the Other Side or another dimension. If you look at them, they are perfectly positioned to be an energetic portal where energy both comes and goes.

There was a time in a past dimension and also in a future dimension, where the pyramids were in use to channel energy from other dimensions. Right now is not that time. There are certain humans who can still feel the energy flowing like a shadow or memory of the past. There are other places that are portals like that as well, like the Bermuda Triangle and Stonehenge. Humanity is working toward having those portals in existence again.

Why don't energetic portals work now like they did in other time periods?

Too many humans at the moment are still very focused on greed. If they were given access to higher energies through energetic portals, it would give more power to the elite and corrupt, which humanity does not need in this physical time. These portals will only open up when the purpose of using them is a loving and positive one. Humans right now would use them for financial gain.

Are we able to explore other dimensions once we return to our non-physical selves on the Other Side?

Yes, once you cross over to the Other Side, you will be able to explore. Where and how far depends on where you are at in your learning journey as a soul. The possibilities for growth are infinite when you are on the Other Side.

Why is Earth positioned where it is in our galaxy?

The answer to this question is simple, yet complex. Simply put, everything works perfectly together. Why does a tree grow up from the ground with its leaves hanging down? Why does grass grow the way it does? Why does water flow the way it does? None of that would happen if the galaxy wasn't positioned exactly how it is. Higher energies and the higher consciousness that created the reality humans live in are infinite engineers who have the ability to perfectly construct anything and everything in existence.

Does Peter have any words of wisdom for those going through trials and tribulations?

A trial or tribulation in your eyes is just a quick lesson from the perspective of the Other Side. What you learn from those experiences is what matters.

Each soul's journey is deeply personal and may involve a complex interplay of factors. While going through trials and tribulations can be challenging, it is an opportunity for the soul to tap into its inherent power, rewrite narratives, and manifest its true potential.

As you navigate your own journey, trust in your inner wisdom, resilience, and the innate worthiness of your soul. Seek support from like-minded individuals, mentors, or spiritual practices which will help you connect with your authentic power. Remember, tough experiences do not define you, but serve as a catalyst for your extraordinary growth and the realization of your infinite nature and everlasting connection to the Other Side.

Can Peter speak on spiritually gifted people?

In order to continue existing, humans need a sense of hope about the future. So every once in a while, the Other Side will take away human amnesia in someone so that person can share their spiritual knowledge and give humanity hope.

Spiritually gifted individuals possess unique abilities and insights which have the power to inspire and uplift humanity. Whether their gifts involve intuitive knowing, healing energy, artistic gifts, musical gifts, or profound wisdom, among many others, it can feel like a guiding light in a world that sometimes feels shrouded in darkness.

Throughout history, these spiritually gifted people have been condemned, they've been celebrated, they've been hated, and they've been loved. Sometimes, they've even found themselves facing persecution and oppression due to complex and varied influences by societal, cultural, and religious factors—most commonly the fear of the unknown.

Yet, society continues to evolve and is beginning to cultivate an environment that respects and celebrates diverse spiritual beliefs and practices. By promoting acceptance, understanding, and compassion, humans can work toward a world where everyone feels safe and loved.

What can we do to help with ascension and the collective enlightenment?

Simply living every day in a human body with human energy progresses the overall enlightenment of humanity.

It might be tempting to believe that in a society where spirituality is often equated with the connection to the Other Side, those who are more spiritually inclined are making the greatest impact. However, this is not always true. Sometimes, it's the individuals who humans would suspect are doing the least who are actually helping the most. These people are often labeled as a "waste"—the ones who are dealing with crippling addiction, living a criminal life in and out of jail, or are just generally outcasts. These people are the ones contributing to collective enlightenment more than some of the most spiritual people in the world. So, you really have to look at it from a broader lens or higher perspective and take away that human impulse to judge in order to really understand it.

Does hell exist?

No. Hell implies a space where we are stuck. Our souls are never stuck. When we die, we all go to the same place.

As an aside, my grandma, who was a devout member of the Church of Jesus Christ of Latter-Day Saints, passed away some time ago. Once, when I was in deep meditation, she came to me in spirit. She appeared so clearly and said, "You know, Amber, you were right. I was shocked when I got here. Everything you said about the Other Side is true." That experience really cemented for me that this is how the Other Side really works. I mean, if my devout grandma who was so convinced of hell and the idea that we had to prove ourselves to get into heaven says to me that she was wrong, it really speaks to me.

Are "bad" people punished when they die?

Humans like to believe bad people will be punished. Many religious doctrines teach us that we will be judged by God when we die. Thankfully, that is just not true. Concepts like these are created by humans for humans in order to create some semblance of control at a time when humans were really corrupt and running amuck. That's not to say Jesus didn't exist, he did. There were also many other wonderful souls that walked the Earth the way he did. It just didn't quite happen the way many of us were taught.

The label of "bad" doesn't exist on the Other Side. Humans could be classified as evil or bad, but at no time does their soul mirror that. All souls are innately good. What lessons are planned in each life have no ability to affect that goodness. There is no need for punishment as your souls do not do what your human self does.

Chapter 13

Guidance from Gayle

A Soul's Heartbeat

How do I see you?

What do I feel?

Your energy radiates and I absorb it.

Your experiences flow through you as clear as a heartbeat.

Up and down, in and out.

Each day adds a new vibration.

Every experience creates a new whole.

*All of your hurt, pain, joy, knowledge, competes
for space, becomes a new beat.*

There is no place where you begin and end.

One glance and you are understood.

There is no judgment, only acceptance.

You came into this world with a uniquely beating heart.

*You will leave this place with a heartbeat
stronger than it has ever been.*

MUCH LIKE A grandmother with a lifetime of timeless wisdom, my spirit guide Gayle is here to offer her insight and advice. What you will read next are her channeled responses to some of our burning questions.

What is the purpose of life and how does it work?

We plan our lives to gain energetic enlightenment through earthly lessons. There is a limit to what we can experience on the Other Side, so life is created to take in all of the things we crave to learn. Each life focuses on different themes of lessons, and we have the ability to experience infinite lives in order to learn. As an example, one of Amber's main themes is patience, which means she will be presented with infinite opportunities to practice patience. Sometimes she will succeed and sometimes she will feel like she's failing, but both are equally important when it comes to her soul's growth.

What are Spirit Guides?

Spirit guides are non-physical beings or energies that assist and guide humanity and individuals on their spiritual journey. They have lived infinite human lives and are now dedicated to helping other humans. Throughout life, they are there communicating through signs, symbols, intuition, dreams, and synchronicities. Our guides are always with us. Picture them as a cheering squad, celebrating every moment of your life. They help us plan our life, they help us live it, then they help us debrief after we die.

What is the difference between an older soul and younger soul?

Everything is created by energy and carries a certain energetic frequency. Energetic frequency, from a spiritual perspective, refers to the vibrational energy that permeates all aspects of existence. It is the underlying energetic signature that contributes to the quality and essence of each living thing.

Amber often refers to this idea of frequency by comparing it to a dimmer switch on a light in your home. The brighter the light, the higher the frequency. The dimmer the light, the lower the frequency. How high or low your frequency is indicates your soul age. Those with the brightest frequency are the souls who have been in existence for the longest period of time, making them old souls.

When trying to wrap your head around this, remember we are not talking about time-based age. An old soul has simply existed and experienced more lifetimes than a younger soul. An older soul is at a stage in their enlightenment where they are choosing to walk through more challenging, painful experiences in life. They often are the ones confronting people, situations, and things that almost break them. It's set up this way not to punish them, but because their soul wants to experience these things to help them continue learning and growing. You can think of the older souls like the students pursuing Master's degrees or a PhD in the spiritual realm.

A younger soul has not existed as long, and is just starting to go through different human lifetimes. A younger soul usually has lower levels of empathy and is consumed mostly by material things, like making a lot of money, buying a huge house, or buying really trendy clothes. They may encounter a few challenges, but their life tends to be pretty easy for the most part. This doesn't mean they are bad people; they are learning just like the rest of humanity. Young souls just happen to be in more beginner "classes" in the spiritual realm.

Most humans fall somewhere in-between. There is no good or bad, better or worse. All souls are just going through this experience called life.

How do you know if you're an old soul?

You can see it in their eyes. An old soul has old eyes. Even as a child, you can look into their eyes and it's like you're looking at a friend. They understand things beyond what you think they should. As they get older, they may feel like their human body just feels more uncomfortable and cumbersome. Yet, the wisdom they carry only grows.

Old souls often look at themselves in the mirror and don't recognize themselves. They may say their name out loud and ask themselves how and why they are in this body. It is more difficult for an old soul to clearly see themselves as human. They are always questioning the reasons why they are here, what they are supposed to be doing, and why they don't feel completely centered in this human body. Often it can feel like an out-of-body experience when chaos erupts around them.

Most old souls unknowingly are focusing on the lessons of themselves and those around them. This leaves them feeling slightly purposeless when they can't identify what those lessons are. An old soul only has to look inside to realize they don't have to have all the answers in this human life. It is okay to feel a little bit lost.

Is soul age the same thing as human age?

No, soul age is a completely separate thing than human age. Human age is measured in years. Soul age is measured in energetic frequency.

How much can we raise our vibration in one lifetime?

Let's say the span of human energy goes from 1 to 10, with 1 being the lowest and 10 being the highest. When you plan your life, your soul sets an intention to raise your energetic vibration within a certain range, which is usually relatively small. So, for instance, your soul may plan to go from 1 to 2. Or from 3 to 4. It's not a lot. You can't go from a young soul to an old soul in one life.

Your higher self is aware of how much energetic growth can be achieved in one life and the souls generally stick to that. If humans try to extend that range in order to manifest things or get greater access to their guides, it almost always creates or amplifies health issues or mental illness because the human is accessing energy the soul didn't intend to. It can also cause some people to become too dependent on the Other Side and their spirit guides to answer every question and to solve every problem, which can become confusing.

Do each of our lives have the same personality?

No, each human life has a unique personality and walks their own unique path. However, no matter which lifetime you look at, you will always carry personality traits and characteristics of your soul. Your soul is always a part of you.

Again, I'm going to use Amber as an example. When she crossed over to the Other Side, there was a whole group of people standing and observing. Each of them was one of her other lives. There were men, women, and children from every life status and every culture in existence. All of these lives are interconnected and she carries a piece of them within her now.

Our higher self is the same. It evolves and learns but doesn't transform into a completely different entity. Over time, it will undergo a wide range of human experiences in various lifetimes with different personalities. But it's essence remains constant.

What happens if we meet another version or part of our soul during our lifetime?

Amber has talked about how this life is kind of like a hologram and each of you plans your life perfectly with everything you need. It is a real phenomenon that exists for everyone—an experience of your own design. Even Amber created her life and everyone in it. Each human she encounters is put there for her to learn, just like all of those humans are there to learn from her.

Everything is planned perfectly on the Other Side. The higher self knows how each life they create is going to play out and how to keep each of these lives apart. No human will know if another version of their soul is in their life until they return to the afterlife, even if they sense that another person might be connected to them on a higher level.

Again, I'll draw on an example from Amber. She is very connected to another life she is living in the southern states right now, yet she knows she will never meet her. Her higher self knows how to separate these two lives. Even in saying this, I am aware this concept is above most humans' comprehension, and having this knowledge does not necessarily help humans move forward in this physical time.

Do we plan different lives where we are of other genders, races, and social classes in order to become more understanding of what it may be like for others?

Souls will plan every type of life multiple times. You will plan a life where you are a murderer and a life where you are murdered. You will plan a life where you are an abuser and a life where you are abused. You will plan lives as every gender and you will plan lives to experience every culture. You will plan lives where you base your existence on religion as well as experiencing a life without faith. A human needs to see life from all angles in order to grow and learn. Some people get hung up on this and hyper focus on the fact they do not ever want to be a murderer or an abuser, etc. Rest assured, you will never be forced to do or plan anything you are not ready for. We go into each life with our eyes wide open and full knowledge of what we are capable of.

Are our spirit guides ever loved ones who have passed on before us?

It is rare. Very occasionally, there will be people who will go directly to the Other Side and become guides, but they usually will not guide their family. They will become spirit guides for other humans who are going through life experiences that they are familiar with or have walked through themselves in a past life.

This doesn't mean your loved ones aren't walking with you and supporting you. They are always there for you to talk to and they always listen. They just aren't as likely to help change your path because that is not their purpose. Just like your guides, they can send signs and symbols to show you they are always with you.

Will there be a more peaceful Earth or a more tumultuous Earth in the coming decades?

Both. Humanity is more peaceful, although humans might see the opposite because they watch the media and see everything in the moment as it happens. If you look back 200 years ago or 300 years ago, a lot of this bad stuff was happening then too. Humans just didn't know about it. So as far as humanity goes, it will get more peaceful as people become more loving and enlightened.

As far as the Earth goes, more tumultuous. Humanity hasn't done much to heal her; Earth is now working on healing herself. In order for her to heal herself, unfortunately she has to end the lives of some humans that are overextending her. That is why humans are seeing so many natural disasters. The Earth knows how to take care of herself, even if we struggle to understand the reasoning.

Through pain comes growth. There may be fires that decimate a forest, but if you look closely, the growth that happens after the fire is more beautiful than what was there before. Humanity has struggled since the beginning of time to manage their needs with the needs of the collective enlightenment or the collective consciousness. The vast majority of humans cannot see the damage we are doing by living in excess. The Earth is slowly bringing it to the forefront.

Why do people say we are awakening as humankind?

Humans are definitely moving forward collectively as a higher, enlightened consciousness. It is a painfully slow process in human based time. More and more humans are being born with the awareness of the suffering of others. Stories and news spread throughout the world very quickly now, so humans cannot deny the pain of the world. All of this contributes to the collective consciousness of enlightenment.

Can we change our exit date or when we die?

Your human self doesn't get to choose most of the time, other than something like suicide. The choice is made by your higher self in partnership with your guides. Each life has a planned beginning and a planned end, and your soul knows how it will happen—an accident, a tragedy, or sickness. And in each life, we will all plan anywhere from two to ten exit points.

These are created so our soul can go back to the Other Side for different reasons, such as your plate is too full or empty, you learned more quickly than you thought you would, you feel off track, or you just want to go home, among many other reasons. Your human self will not be aware of these exit points. That is all thought of before you came into this world.

When you are on the Other Side, do you retain the memories of all your human lives?

Yes, you do. I will use Amber as an example. The moment she crossed over, she could not only feel her other lives, but she innately knew everything they went through. When you cross over, the human amnesia you are born with is gone in an instant. You understand every aspect of your higher self and all at once, you can see and feel every other existence you have experienced.

Do negative energies exist and can we protect ourselves from them?

There are humans who carry a lower energetic frequency. They can be a bit of a nuisance sometimes, but that is where you can set a boundary and protect yourself as much as you can. As far as souls on the Other Side, there is no Hell, but there are lower energy spirits. Sometimes, they come through here on Earth to apologize to humans they hurt here, but they aren't suffering on the Other Side. That energy can join back up with their higher self anytime.

How can we get more in tune with our higher self?

Humans are born in tune with their higher selves. Most of the time, they forget that connection and that's okay. But if you are a human who craves developing that connection again, you only need to have faith in yourself, your higher self, and your guides. Spend time in stillness, focusing on the home you have come from on the Other Side, and the learning you are doing now. Try to not focus on what you feel you are lacking, but rather be grateful for the infinite power of free will.

If our souls plan everything, why would we choose a life that hurts so bad?

All souls are on a journey of growth and expansion. Through experiences of pain and suffering, you are able to gain profound insights, wisdom, and spiritual growth. When you are creating your life plan on the Other Side, your soul may intentionally choose life experiences that are especially challenging in order to learn what it feels like to hurt, and to develop qualities like resilience, compassion, forgiveness, and empathy.

This is important because souls are not able to learn a lot of those lessons on the Other Side, hence why we plan a human life. On the Other Side, all souls know is love. So, they create life and incarnate on this planet with purpose. As humans live out their life, they will be faced with that which makes them the most fearful, challenged, or angry. Souls will intentionally set things up so they will run into people who will challenge their self-worth, make them anxious, and get on their every nerve. This is done by design not to punish you, but to help your soul evolve. Remember, there is no passing or failing in this process. It's about how humans walk through these experiences, process it, and make peace with it that matters.

May you find solace in knowing that all humans are helping one another learn, even in the midst of pain. Just by being alive, you are contributing more to the collective than you might realize.

Why don't we remember planning our life or being on the Other Side before we were born?

Depending on the human, somewhere between ages one and five, you forget that connection to the Other Side. You no longer experience that peaceful, wonderful feeling of "Yes, I planned this and everything is going to be okay." It's called human amnesia, and most humans choose to have it. Once in a while, there are people like Amber who still retain some of that memory. These are the ones we usually refer to as psychics, mediums, empaths, healers, artists, musicians, and creatives.

And sometimes, people have life experiences that take away the human amnesia they were born with. One example is people with Alzheimer's disease. When they get near the end of their life, their soul may choose to access the love on the Other Side in order to alleviate the fear and pain they experience.

What is the purpose of anxiety and depression?

Anxiety and depression are fairly heavy energetic feelings. Souls who have chosen a more challenging life often want to experience these difficulties. In learning about and focusing on heavier human emotions, you contribute to the collective consciousness in a deeper way than a human who only experiences joy. And as your soul ages, you become more and more capable of walking through heavier lessons. You may also become more empathic, which can manifest as anxiety and depression. Through our eyes on the Other Side, although we can see you are experiencing pain, we also can see the benefits of the enlightenment of the collective consciousness.

What if people hurt you unknowingly, but you are very aware?

Finding yourself in a situation like this can be deeply challenging, often serving as a huge spiritual lesson. It is so much harder when someone hurts us without knowledge of the pain they have caused, as they may never apologize.

It is important to remember that awareness and understanding can vary among individuals, and sometimes people may cause harm without realizing it or acknowledging it. In these moments, honor your own feelings and experiences. Acknowledge the pain and hurt that you have endured, regardless of whether the other person is aware or not. Your emotions are valid, and it is essential to prioritize your own healing and well-being.

While it is natural to desire acknowledgement and understanding from those who hurt you, it is important to release expectations and detach from the outcome. The journey of healing and growth is a lengthy one, and should not depend on someone else but on your own commitment to self-care and inner transformation. You have to learn how to make peace within yourself and cleanse the pain from your soul. Not easy. But it opens the door to so much growth.

How do we know if we are progressing as a soul?

You are making progress as a soul just by breathing. There is nothing you can or can't do to stop your progression. As long as you are breathing, you are learning. Anybody who tells you differently is expressing a very human view. There are no other stipulations. There are no gold stars or benchmarks to meet. Even someone who is comatose, spending years lying in a bed, is still learning and walking through the lessons their soul planned.

Does having a high vibration always mean positive emotions and well-being?

No. High vibration and positive emotions don't go hand in hand most of the time. It is hard to be an enlightened person because you feel more and hurt more than most. You are more connected to everything around you, but also more affected by energy—both positive and negative.

Why do people see different things when they have an NDE?

What we believe as humans forms our physical reality and is the glue that holds our world together. Perception really is everything. So let's say you are a very religious person who strongly believes certain things. If you have a near-death experience, you will most likely see a vision that represents your belief system. For some, that might be seeing Jesus. For others, it could be the Buddha. Others might see nothing if they truly believe there is nothing after death. It is set up that way so your human mind can process what's happening and you can return to your physical body and continue your life. Every once in a while, someone might have an NDE and see something that is very different from what they believed before, but that does not happen often. Until you die and completely transition to the Other Side, you won't have any tangible proof of what is true. In the meantime, we only have faith.

Why do some people suffer before they die and others don't?

Our souls can choose to have a death that is very physically or mentally painful or a death which is peaceful and calm. Our souls will all choose to go through every type of death in different lifetimes. We will all experience a death that involves something like a plane crash, a car accident, terminal disease, murder, all of it.

The older your soul is, the more extreme it can be. As an older soul, you'll either die in a really awful way or choose to leave your body right before something like that happens so your physical body doesn't have to experience it. Just like everything else, it's a lesson. But the soul never has to die in a way they don't want to. Even if it looks like, from a human perspective, to be unbearable or painful, the soul planned it out with love and with purpose.

Can you heal a past life?

We can't necessarily go back and alter or heal a past life because all of our lives are happening simultaneously; the concept of linear time is an illusion we have created. But, you may be able to increase awareness of a past life, and that might bring you peace just knowing that you can access that part of you through hypnosis or meditation. Psychologically, if you think it will help, it will help.

However, concretely going back to a past life and changing it or healing it, is not really possible nor should it be. All of our lives intertwine infinitely and perfectly. Our souls wouldn't want to change any of them because it would send a wave off into the universe which could change things in the opposite way we intended.

Is the law of attraction a real thing?

Yes. We attract things through energy, and our thoughts and emotions emit energetic vibrations which interact with the universe. These vibrations, whether positive or negative, align with similar vibrations in the universe and attract corresponding experiences, people, or circumstances into our lives. We are definitely co-creators of our reality. So if you are carrying resentment, anxiety, or anger, you'll continue to be faced with things that provoke those feelings.

On the Other Side, your higher self and guides are watching and will say, "Oh, they're really focusing on that. She must be learning. Let's give her more of that so she can face it and hopefully overcome it." They never do this as punishment, but present these opportunities with love. They have faith that you can handle them and know how rewarding it will feel when you overcome even the biggest challenges.

If you ever find yourself in a tough scenario and you're not sure what to do, try looking for the lesson. Try taking a step back and reflecting on the question, "I'm really struggling right now. What are the lessons I'm walking through?" If you can identify the lessons and understand why you're stuck there, your guides and higher self may ease up a bit if they see you're getting it.

Many humans may struggle with this concept because we get almost addicted to the chaos. We get uncomfortable when we don't have it. I can get that way too. I can get really down on myself and ask, "What is going on? Why am I doing this? Why did I choose this?" I fully know that I should be identifying the lessons so my guides can work with me instead of throwing more lessons my way. But sometimes I like to sit in a toddler temper tantrum position and say, "Screw that. Nope! I want to be upset right now." It's human to get frustrated sometimes. But you just have to identify the lessons in order to start to move past them.

What is an example of a life lesson our soul might choose to learn?

Within the realm of life lessons, souls may choose to embark on various experiences to facilitate their growth and spiritual evolution. These lessons can encompass a wide range of themes, challenges, and opportunities for learning.

One possible life lesson a soul might choose is the experience of forgiveness and letting go of resentment. Imagine a soul that carries deep-seated anger and resentment from past experiences. They may have encountered many situations where they were hurt, betrayed, or felt unjustly treated.

In their current incarnation, the soul may choose to learn the transformative power of forgiveness and release. They may attract challenging relationships or circumstances that mirror the wounds they carry, providing them with ample opportunities to confront their unresolved emotions. Throughout their journey, this soul encounters individuals who trigger their wounds and evoke intense anger. What at first glance might seem like hell, is actually a chance for the soul to heal and grow by consciously choosing forgiveness and compassion instead of perpetuating cycles of pain and negativity.

By navigating these experiences and embracing forgiveness, the soul learns to free themselves from the burden of resentment and reclaim their inner peace. They realize that forgiveness is not about condoning the actions of others, but rather a profound act of self-liberation and spiritual growth.

It's important to remember that life lessons are deeply personal and tailored to each soul's unique journey. This example provided is just one illustration of the countless possibilities for soul growth and evolution. There are infinite combinations of themes we can choose, such as empathy, patience, balance, caregiving, anxiety, self-worth, etc.

Dealing with Loss

Navigating loss and the profound experience of death can be a deeply challenging and transformative journey. Grief is a human and natural response, and can stir up a myriad of emotions and disrupt our sense of stability and well-being. It's essential to honor and acknowledge these emotions, allowing yourself the space to grieve in your own way and at your own pace. It's a journey of healing that takes time, and it's okay to honor your own process, even if it looks different from what society or others expect. Trust your inner wisdom and follow the path that feels true to you.

From a spiritual perspective, death is a beautiful transition—a passage from one form of existence to another. Our souls never really die; we simply continue living on the Other Side where we are reunited with our family, our loved ones, and our pets. The people you've lost in your life are still with you, and are still loving you, even years after their physical body is gone. Just as much as you want to know if they are okay, they want to make sure you are okay too.

After all, death reminds us of the impermanence of life and encourages us to treasure each moment and relationship.

It invites us to live with greater presence and appreciation, cultivating gratitude for the experiences and connections we have in the here and now.

Miscarriages and Stillbirths

A lot of people ask me the question, "If I miscarried a baby or experienced a stillbirth, is that baby still cared for on the Other Side?" My answer is always yes. Your higher self and your family are always there. We are never alone on the Other Side. No one is ever left on their own on the Other Side to struggle. They are always loved and cared for, even more than we are here. It is also important to note that our souls choose each life and death, so if you lose a child, both of your souls would have planned it.

The other thing worth mentioning is that souls will often continue to try to come back to you if they are miscarried, stillborn, or aborted. For example, if you have suffered multiple miscarriages, it will usually be the same soul trying to come into your life. This doesn't always happen, but it is very common. And occasionally, the soul will wait for another opportunity to incarnate. In this case, they might become your second child. All of this is agreed upon before you come into this life. You choose your children, when, and if, they will be born. You don't tell them or order them, they have to agree to each life as well.

Chapter 14

A Comforting Chat with Jessica

Unapologetic Laughter

What makes you truly happy?

Is it a hot drink on a cold day, a kind word
from a friend, sand between your toes?

This life is not all learning, pain and strife.

There is always time to focus on the joy we
can achieve throughout our lives.

Happiness gives balance to the deep
learning we plan into each life.

There is no better stress relief than laughter.

So take time to have that drink, have a chat with a friend,
pause, and breathe, with sand between your toes.

Each life is a balancing act of what it means to be human.

Your higher self and guides love you more
than you could ever know.

They will laugh with you, they will revel in the
joy you consciously bring into your life.

So celebrate yourself and your growth in this life.

Laugh unapologetically and often. You have earned it.

WHAT FOLLOWS NEXT are conversations between me and my spirit guide Jessica, where we dive into more of life's mysteries. Some of these questions are answered by Jessica, some by me and others are a combination of both of us. Jessica is similar to me when it comes to views and opinions.

Is X, Y, Z a sign from your guides?

Numbers, feathers, dimes, butterflies, hummingbirds. So many people want a concrete sign. Unfortunately, when you are really focusing on receiving a sign, you may miss it. More often than not, spirit guides send signs when humans are having a really difficult time. They don't usually do it just for fun or encouragement, although that can still happen. If you're a fairly functioning human, you may not get signs ever. They give us signs when we need them, not when we want them. The exception to this is signs from our loved ones who have crossed over. They enjoy sending signs randomly, so we know they are thinking of us and are always near. With a little bit of faith, hopefully you will see and understand the signs your loved ones and guides are sending.

How I communicate with spirit guides

Before my stroke, when I wanted to communicate with my spirit guides I would have to ask a question, pause and listen for the answer, then speak. Every once in a while, I'd have to ask clarifying questions if I didn't understand what was coming through or if I didn't want to say something. I was continuously worried about how the other person might react. Sometimes my guides are much more blunt than me personally.

Now, it's all telepathic. They think, and I speak. There's no delay. It's almost like we're sharing the same mind. When I do my meditation before a reading or spiritual work, I just say, "I want your voice to become my words. I want it to be clear, concise, and without confusion." I just invite them to come and sit with me. They're always to the right of me, standing there. I'm more of just a direct channel.

A warning about communicating with spirit guides

Communicating with spirit guides can be a beautiful experience. But it's not something that should be overdone. We have to remember we are spiritual beings walking through a human experience, and we created this life with the intention of making decisions and figuring it out on our own.

What makes it challenging is that, as our society opens up to spirituality, people are encouraged to tap in and connect with spirit guides for everything. It can become addictive. When you're being guided by them, it can feel like you have a magic 8 ball or some sort of secret gift that allows you to see into the future and predict what's going to happen. While it's 100% possible to get a glimpse of the future or accurately predict things, it can also give us a false sense of control. Free will exists and the future as we might see it is guaranteed to no one. We aren't here to know everything, and if we become too reliant on the Other Side to give us all the answers, it takes us out of the present moment and creates a life where we become consumed by anticipating what will happen next instead of just enjoying what is.

It's funny because when I first accepted my spiritual gifts

years ago, people used to say to me, "Oh, you're so lucky. If I could, I'd be talking to my guides all the time. Amber, why don't you use yours to figure out what happened to this famous person, or get the winning lottery numbers?" But the truth is, outside of work I rarely ask my spirit guides for guidance. When I do need their support in my personal life, I just say, "I have so much gratitude that you're walking with me as I make these decisions." I've learned that they aren't here to give me all the answers. They are energetic beings that are meant to walk beside us to make sure we don't fall as we're living our life and making decisions.

I know hearing this might sound strange because I make a living off of people coming to me for spiritual guidance. But, when I do an intuitive reading for somebody, their spirit guides help them recognize what they're struggling with. They don't fix everything for that person, they give homework so they can learn how to do it themself.

The truth is, not all of us need to have an energetic or spiritually based life. All of our souls already know how to do that on the Other Side. We come here to learn everything else.

Tools for communicating with the Other Side

When it comes to communicating with the Other Side, there are various tools and practices you can explore to enhance your connection. A few commonly used tools and approaches to consider might be divination tools like tarot cards, oracle cards, or pendulums. I personally like tapping in through meditation. Meditation is a powerful practice for quieting the mind and opening up to spiritual insights. By entering a calm and focused state, you create a conducive environment for connecting with the spiritual realm. Make sure to keep in mind, the energy you carry can affect your connection, so always cleanse and protect before any spiritual work.

When we are channeling the Other Side, is it normal for different beings to communicate differently?

It depends on which energetic frequency they are. Spirit guides have experienced human life before, and they usually can communicate with us very easily and clearly. On the flip side, if we try to tap in and communicate with a loved one who passed away, but is carrying a lower energetic frequency, communication can get harder and more confusing. Think of it this way: on this planet there are people who make sense to you, people you get along with well, and friends you can talk with for hours and it feels like seconds. Then there are other people that you spend five minutes with, and you don't understand them, you don't agree with what they're saying, and the whole thing just feels exhausting and you don't enjoy it. It's the same on the Other Side. Some energies come through very clearly and others can be harder to feel or understand.

Do we still have a connection with our pets and animals after they die?

Yes. Animals often consider us their heaven. When they pass over, they go to the same place on the Other Side as we do, but they often return to check on us.

What is super unique, especially about dogs, cats, and horses is that their souls can continue to reincarnate into your life over and over and over. They might not come back as the same breed or with the same physical appearance, but their soul will return to you. Just like humans, animals have a higher self or soul that is like a rain cloud that produces raindrops (lives.) They can plan to have numerous experiences living with you. They come here like a little piece from the Other Side to remind us what that true loving energy feels like.

I remember when I was thirteen or fourteen, I got my first dog and man oh man was he my soul dog at that time. Eventually he got old and passed away, but when I was twenty, I got a chihuahua who was exactly like my first dog. She was a completely different breed and didn't look like him at all, but her energy and the way I felt around her was so similar. Of course, after a few years she got very old and crossed over. But after that, I got another dog named Walter who was definitely another soul dog. I had the closest bond with him, more than any other animal. Even after he was gone, I could still hear his footsteps in our living room and sense him or smell him sometimes. Walter passed away right around the time I had my stroke, but just recently we adopted a new puppy and I can already tell he's a "raindrop" or part of Walter's soul who incarnated again. That is what the cycle looks like for a lot of animals. They will keep coming back to us because they're so bonded to our souls.

Keep in mind that not every animal will choose to reincarnate. Some may cross over to the Other Side and choose, for whatever reason, not to come back. For example, if an animal is abused or not treated very well, they won't come back to that person or that family again. They usually are only in those situations to help teach humans how to love and teach what the absence of love looks like. Sometimes, even if an animal was treated well and never experienced abuse, they still won't reincarnate simply because they choose not to. Each situation and each animal life is unique.

When you do have a soul animal in your life, you'll be able to tell. With soul animals, it's just obvious how much they love us and how much they love being around us. You'll recognize their energy. For instance, with my new puppy, from the moment we got him it was like he already knew me. He puts his little head in my hand and looks up at me like, "Ahh, I'm finally back." And he just looks so happy. It's a soul connection.

Is it okay to go to tarot card readers?

If you go to a tarot reader, you have to make sure their energy is light and positive and vibes with yours. If it feels sluggish or kind of off, you may not get an accurate representation of where you are on your spiritual path. I suggest looking at reviews, watching videos, reading their profile, and feeling their energy. Have they been helpful? For me, I get a lot of comments of "I feel like I know you" or "You're so calming." Avoid hectic or questionable energy when trying to seek out spiritual guidance.

Are Ouija boards evil?

Ouija boards aren't evil, but there's a bit of a dark connotation to them. It doesn't have to do so much with the Other Side, though. Our loved ones will do almost anything to let us know that they're there for us. The darkness has more to do with the kind of energy people are bringing into the space when they use them. For instance, if someone is experiencing a lot of fear and anxiety around using a Ouija board, they'll likely feel fear and anxiety. But if you have really good energy and have crystals around like selenite and maybe obsidian, it could be okay.

The Ouija board can be a good tool to have a conversation with passed over loved ones if you have that capability. It's not dark magic. It's not of the devil. It's just "user beware" because not everyone should use it, especially if you're under the influence of any substances. So use with caution and with really loving energy.

Can you speak on religion and conflicting belief systems?

They show it to me like this: you know in school where you played the game telephone? You sit in a circle and one person would whisper something to someone, that person would pass it to the next, and by the time it got to the end of the circle, the original message had turned into something completely different? This is similar to what happened to a lot of religious teachings. Many of the stories are real and true. But these messages were passed down during a time when humanity needed reward and punishment in order to exist. These stories have been written down and adapted so many times. What humanity needs today and how people are interpreting these ancient texts has changed, and may continue to change throughout time.

What if I don't want to reincarnate on Earth again?

It's not uncommon for humans who are struggling right now to cringe at the thought of coming back and living another life. But your soul sees life as exciting. Your soul wants the opportunity to learn and grow as much as it can. That is sometimes hard for humans to understand. Humans might even think to themselves, "Well, that's messed up. Why would our souls want us to struggle or experience pain?" But pain doesn't feel like pain when you're on the Other Side. It just feels like a lesson. Our souls have a completely different way of looking at things.

If you don't want to plan a life or live a life, you will never be forced to. The decision is always up to you. However, for many souls, they experience a strong desire to reincarnate and deeply want to come back. It's thrilling coming into each life knowing all the things you'll get to learn and experience. It's part of the journey to enlightenment.

How do we balance being a human and a spiritual being having a human experience?

You don't have to. You are already innately balanced. Even if you feel unbalanced, your soul is always okay and never unwell or unsteady.

Why are so many people experiencing financial anxiety right now?

This is one of the most common life lessons for many humans. It is something I've struggled with my entire life. I am fully aware it's something within me that I have to figure out. Sometimes when I sit back in private reflection, I'll ask myself why I'm like this. I'll try and think about where this comes from. And then it hits me…I was mostly raised poor. I was out on my own at fifteen years old, juggling school and a full-time job, and I never had enough. Half of my teeth rotted out of my head because I couldn't afford to fix them.

Now as an adult, I constantly worry about having enough for myself and to provide for my kids. This feeling of financial anxiety has ingrained in me from early on. I recognize the pattern and know what it is, but it doesn't stop me from freaking out. It's helped me to remember that money doesn't buy happiness.

Overcoming Fear

Before I accepted my spiritual gifts, whenever I started to experience fear and anxiety, I would outright avoid it (which usually meant getting completely consumed in cleaning anything and everything.) The downside of this was I didn't really fix anything, I just put it off. I've learned from my guides that the treatment for the feeling of anxiety is to face that which makes you the most fearful, which sounds horrific, but does really work. I know it has in my own life.

When I had my stroke, they took away my driver's license and told me I might never be able to drive again. But after a year, I finally felt well enough to re-apply for it, so I took the driver's test and got approved! Since then, I've driven a few times with my husband Mike in the car, but haven't driven alone. It's scary to think about getting in the car by myself because it makes me so anxious. I know it's going to be uncomfortable and my heart is going to be beating really hard and it's going to be difficult, but I'm going to do it anyway.

Doing it means that the next time, I probably won't be as scared. Instead of feeling like I'm at a level 10 anxiety level, maybe it will be at a level 9. The next time after that, maybe it will drop to 5. Hopefully it will just keep dropping until it becomes a part of my everyday life.

The day I got my license back, December 28ᵗʰ, 2022

I think it's only human to avoid what makes us uncomfortable. I mean, someone with social anxiety might get really uncomfortable when they're around more than five people at a time, so they might avoid large groups. Or maybe someone gets really anxious when they try new things, so they stick to what they know. It's easy to avoid everything, especially when it affects our nervous system so deeply. But sometimes it's good to get pushed out of your comfort zone.

Overcoming fear is a transformative journey that requires self-awareness, determination, and a willingness to embrace growth. You can start small with a gradual approach that allows you to build confidence and momentum. Start with activities or situations that are slightly challenging but manageable. Celebrate each small achievement, as it reinforces your progress and boosts your confidence. Remind yourself that sometimes the greatest achievements often lie on the other side of fear.

Anger

Anger serves a purpose as it holds us in lessons. I've had many situations in my personal life where I've been angry with people. I had trouble talking about it, and I would just let it stew. I used to carry anger around with me all the time, every day. Now I'm better at talking to people when I'm frustrated with them, but it's something I'm still working on. Anger kept me in those lessons of forgiveness, learning how it affects me, and how it was preventing me from moving forward. In a way, that's really, really, good soul growth. It's a way to force us to learn the lessons we don't want to learn, but will benefit our souls. From our human perspective, though, it sucks. Anger is probably the hardest emotion to carry.

It's interesting because there is almost always something underneath the anger. Anger is like a protective blanket that helps to keep you from experiencing the more vulnerable, raw emotions like sadness, betrayal, or fear. While it's easy to get caught in negative feelings, by exploring our underlying emotions we can understand what fuels our anger so we can address it and find a better way to cope.

Sometimes we feel anger because we're at the base level of learning some really difficult lessons and we're supposed to stay there. It's something your soul wants to experience and grow from. I'd like to say that everyone can learn these lessons and wake up tomorrow feeling better, but that's just not the case. If you are waking up and you are angry every day for no reason, try to figure out why. Talk to someone. Ask for help.

It's important to remember that we all are completely in control of how we react to situations and how we feel, no matter what. This lesson can be a hard pill to swallow, especially after you've been wronged or hurt by someone else. You might be thinking, "This person mistreated me for years and now I'm angry. I should be able to blame them for that." Yes, that person mistreated you for years. That mistreatment is their fault. But letting it continue to affect you, that is something you can work on overcoming. This will help you find inner peace and acceptance about what happened. Go back to the moment of abuse and take back control. The anger comes from a feeling of being out of control, like someone stole something from you. Forgive the person, forgive yourself. A lot of the time we blame ourselves for some weird reason. Forgive. Forgive. Forgive.

If you're around people and they're super angry, it's okay to remove yourself. Sometimes I say to people, "Oh, your energy is not good for me. I have to go." Emotions are contagious, especially for empaths, and anger is a particularly potent energy that can quickly permeate our own state of being. When we remain in the vicinity of intense anger, we risk absorbing that negative energy, which can impact our own emotional well-being and create unnecessary stress. By stepping away, we prioritize our mental and emotional health, giving ourselves the opportunity to regain a sense of calm and balance.

How can we move past hurtful situations?

If you can try to be grateful to be presented with all the wonderful learning opportunities, they may not affect you as much. Every day you get to choose how you approach the world. How you act. How you feel. Nobody else does that for you. Nobody is above it. It is a part of the human experience. Struggling is learning. Every moment was planned with love. Life is perfect in its imperfection.

If you desire to manifest a different experience, you can. Have you ever seen the commercials with the people living on the beach in a really cool van? They wake up every morning to the warm sun on their face and a cup of delicious coffee in their hand. They truly exude happiness. They love their life and have gratitude for everything in it. And they're bringing all these wonderful people and opportunities into their lives. That's like the gold standard of saying, "You know what? I'm going to create joy even if I'm feeling shitty." Before you know it, it will manifest into your life.

Is it possible to fail at life?

Nope, never. Human life is treasured on the Other Side. We love walking with our human body and learning lessons. Each life is like one small piece of an infinite puzzle with limitless possibilities. From our soul's perspective, it's all a wonderful journey of exploration.

When we look at it from a human point of view, we put a lot of pressure on ourselves. We think we have to do everything and have everything figured out. Societal pressure makes this difficult. In the last five years, humanity has really started to embrace spirituality and has been encouraging people to "Pay attention to your soul. Pay attention to your purpose." But it's still in human terms. So it's gone from "Be successful. Be rich. Have a vacation home." to "Be balanced. Practice joy. Practice self-care." But with the same horrible undertone of, "But if you don't do it, you're not good enough."

That good/bad and pass/fail mentality doesn't make sense to our souls. On the Other Side, we simply seek to learn and experience every aspect of human existence. What most of us might see as a horrible thing, our soul views as an exceptional learning opportunity. To learn is to evolve. You can never do it wrong.

What can we do to help our planet?

On the Other Side, sometimes the higher energies think about the number of times we have had to restart the Earth because humanity has overtaxed the planet. Energies on the Other Side understand that all of it is part of the learning process, but the Earth needs to be cared for in order for the Earth to take care of the people on it. This is one lesson that humanity has yet to fully understand. Be aware of your choices. Every step you make on the Earth has an energetic impact. Learn to focus higher energy when interacting with Mother Earth and treat her with love. Whenever you have a moment, put your bare feet on the ground and express gratitude for the endless energy Mother Earth shares.

How can we impact humanity and the world in a positive way?

Be yourself, be human, be kind, and have gratitude every day. Not enough can be said about kindness. There's been times in history where kindness has been really hard to come by. Humans are making progress with this now, but they get so busy in their daily lives that they may go an entire day without a kind word or a smile to or from another human. Take the time to be kind. It goes a long way.

What is the future of humanity?

For such a long time, humanity has been focused on material success. So many carry this into their own lives and are primarily concerned with taking care of their family and the ones they love so they can survive. As we look into the future, a remarkable transformation is underway—a shift from "me" to "we." It's a shift from an ego-centered value system to one rooted in empathy and collective well-being. This profound societal change reflects an awakening, a recognition of the true evolution of consciousness, where compassion and empathy guide our interactions and shape a brighter future for all of us.

As humanity evolves, we are realizing that empathy is not just a virtue, but a fundamental necessity. The ego-centered mindset, which prioritizes personal success at the expense of others, is giving way to a collective understanding of our interconnectedness. After all, we are all human. Whether you look at race, gender, socio-economic status, or anything else, we are more alike than we are different. We all have to do things to preserve this human existence. There has never been a time where we've been more connected. I mean, we have access to the world at our fingertips. This is opening up an incredible opportunity to bridge divides, foster connection, and promote healing in a world hungry for compassion. Eventually, I see empathy becoming the norm. Not being able to see another person's point of view or really empathize with what's going on for them is going to be viewed as abnormal.

The future lies in embracing the value of shared prosperity, where success is measured not only by personal accomplishments, but by the upliftment and support of others. As we cultivate empathy and shift our focus toward collective well-being, we create more harmonious and compassionate societies. You can see it happening already. Across the globe, inspiring stories of empathy in action are emerging, illustrating the power of compassionate choices to bring about positive change. From grassroots movements to influential change-makers, people are slowly but surely transforming the way we live. I know it might not seem this way right now, but they are there. You might not always hear about it on the news, but if you look closely enough, you'll see good people do exist in this world and there are more of them than you might guess.

And as empathy takes root in our hearts and minds, its transformative influence expands far beyond our personal spheres. It permeates our families, workplaces, educational institutions, and beyond, creating a ripple effect of love and understanding. We have never progressed so rapidly. We now know beyond a shadow of a doubt that what we do affects others. The views we have are not always the same as others and that is okay. We are coming to the understanding people are people and that's it. It is not happening overnight, but we are making more forward progress than we ever had before because we can't hide now. We are so exposed to everything. There are cameras everywhere. You can see everything for yourself, everyday, all day.

As we continue to awaken and evolve, we have the opportunity to create a world that is more loving and harmonious for all beings. This transformative change will solidify a shift in consciousness from a state of separation and individuality to one of unity and interconnectedness. You might have heard this referred to as a spiritual awakening or ascension; the labels do not matter. At its core, the awakening of humanity is about recognizing and experiencing the true nature of our being, which is pure consciousness, divine love, and infinite wisdom. It involves the realization that we are not separate individuals, but rather expressions of the same divine consciousness that brings life to all of creation.

So, let's all continue to nurture the seeds of empathy within ourselves and inspire others to embrace this transformative journey. Together, we can create a world that thrives on compassion and connection.

Chapter 15

Flowers from Heaven

We Are One

Our world feels broken, we are all at war.

No one is exempt, from the rich to the poor.

We use words like weapons, we aim to kill.

Without a thought to the outcome, just the cheap thrill.

No person is spared from the judgment or shame.

We all play a part, we are all to blame.

Our eyes have lost focus, we no longer see,

Every human being is no different from me.

We throw words at each other, labels condemn .

It is no longer we, but rather us and them.

We scream, shout and fight for our rights every day.

We fail to see the high price we must pay.

There is no one among us that is greater than all.

Together we are strong, alone we will fall.

We must open our eyes, before all is lost.

We must see we are equal, no matter the cost.

IT HAS BEEN about sixteen months since the stroke and amazingly, we're at the end of the book. Reflecting on everything I've been through and all that it encompassed, I can honestly say it's something I will never forget. It is truly astonishing to find myself here today because I never thought I would survive. Coming out of this whole thing has me thinking about my future, and I must admit, I have no idea what lies ahead. My inner knowing and spiritual self acknowledge that there are going to be struggles, but I know what is to come will be an experience of a lifetime.

To this day, the things my spirit guides told me when I was on the Other Side are coming to fruition. Things like this book. In about ten weeks, Sara and I got an entire book's worth of information on paper. I still keep thinking, *how*? Writing a book usually takes so much longer.

What a difference a year makes!

I have also started painting. It was one day in mid-April 2023 when my spirit guides said to me, "You need to paint. You need to do watercolor paintings of flowers and scenery from the Other Side." They were very adamant about it being watercolor, although I'm not sure why.

When I first heard them say this, I thought to myself, *um, no. I've never painted anything in my life, not to mention that I have a severe brain injury. How am I supposed to paint when I'm missing two thirds of the left side of my brain?*

So I ignored them for a while and didn't do it. My guides kept bothering me and wouldn't let up. After a few days of them getting on my case about it, I finally gave in and decided to do it. At first, I thought I might have to go out and buy some art supplies, but as it turns out my son had watercolor paints and a few paint brushes left over from a class he took a while back. What he had wasn't anything fancy, it was pretty inexpensive stuff, and I knew that if I tried to paint and it didn't work out we wouldn't really lose anything, so why not give it a shot?

Magically out of nowhere, I could paint! My first watercolor painting turned out beautifully, and I was astonished. When I was on the Other Side, there were meadows everywhere. The painting I created somewhat mirrored the blue flowers I saw while I was there. I couldn't believe my eyes. I remember thinking to myself, *is this really happening? Maybe this first painting was just beginner's luck or some sort of weird fluke.* So I kept going.

Next I tried to capture an image of similar flowers, but this time in yellow. This one turned out just as beautifully and it felt really easy to do. The next few paintings after that just flowed out of me. Each one took me only about fifteen to thirty minutes and were made up of all different colors. I painted roses, tulips, bamboo, and all kinds of stuff. I couldn't stop. It just kept flowing out of my soul. My spirit guides later told me my new ability to paint was a gift given to me on the Other Side as another way for me to express my experiences.

I have decided to call this collection of watercolor paintings Flowers from Heaven because I'm trying my hardest to paint what I saw on the Other Side. I want people to see and feel that energy. It's hard because there were so many colors in the afterlife and it's difficult to really capture how captivating everything looked. Right now, I'm just amazed that I can do it at all. It's miraculous.

Once I had mastered flowers, I started trying to paint some of the many galaxies I had access to on the Other Side. I struggled to create accurate colors, but they still turned out beautifully.

Driven by the urge for perfection, I get lost in the detail, hoping to capture the essence of the flowers I saw on the Other Side.

Trying to capture the indescribable colors of the Other Side.

I call this one 'Flowers from Heaven.'

A vivid recollection of the garden I discovered on the Other Side.

*A galaxy I was inspired to paint post stroke after
being able to access other dimensions.*

It's funny because for a while after my near-death experience, especially in the beginning, I didn't really understand why I ever would have chosen to come back. Everything was so hard. Words can't explain how difficult my life was. But I also remembered my guides telling me that after eighteen months, everything would start taking off. And it just so happened that my book was professionally edited in June, eighteen months after my stroke. I feel so grateful because everything has all come together, just like my guides said it would. It's almost unbelievable.

I have also started to realize the importance of me returning to this physical body not just for my family, but to help teach the collective and bring in a renewed sense of hope and love. That's something else my guides told me would happen. When I was on the Other Side, they explained that my life up to that point was 70% focused on learning and 30% focused on teaching. I was walking through human lessons and understanding more deeply my place in the world and the purpose of all that is. After the stroke, they said I would make a significant shift. Instead of walking through life primarily as a student, they explained that I would come back into my body with the main purpose of teaching. Teaching was going to become so important in my life that I was going to be 80% focused on it. My role would be to share what I learned on the Other Side and to help others understand the purpose of life and find greater meaning in their existence. And let me tell you, it wasn't easy for me to accept.

After my stroke people around me kept saying how inspiring my journey was, but I didn't feel like it was inspiring. It was excruciating and grueling, like I was being tortured every day. But now, I'm starting to see the teaching piece come in more and more. I've started putting myself out there and it's been great. One thing I've especially enjoyed is doing interviews. It's interesting because the podcast hosts are all asking me the same question: "What is the one thing you want people to know about the experience you went through?" And this is the answer I want to leave with everybody:

The Other Side is our home and this is our school. We plan these lives with love, and we do so joyfully and lovingly with the intention of learning certain lessons. I don't think this means we have to 100% understand how it works or focus all our energy on learning every day. In fact, I think it's the opposite. I think it's our job just to be. Just to exist. To simply be in the moment and walk through each experience as it comes into our life. We don't need to try. We just need to allow. Afterall, just breathing is learning. Relationships, connections, jobs, socio-economic status—all of that contributes to the learning. You are exactly where you are meant to be, doing what you're meant to be doing, struggling and working through what your soul intended to experience, and you're doing it beautifully. No matter what happens, you can't get it wrong.

Whatever you are going through in life right now, you're doing it right. In any given situation, on any given day—

whether you're joyful, or sad, or guilty, or shameful—you're doing it right. You're walking through this human life with purpose, with gratitude, even if you don't feel that way right now. Every day that you wake up and breathe, you are learning and you are living your purpose.

And as you're doing all of this, you're never forgotten. There is always a huge support system for you on the Other Side. When I say that, I don't just mean your loved ones who have passed away. Yes, they are there for you without a doubt. Most of the time, our loved ones are quietly observing, offering us love and support. Your higher self and spirit guides are literally cheering in the background of your life every moment you're living it. There is never a time when you are abandoned or uncared for. Even during those moments when you might feel isolated, your guides remain unwavering in their love for you, even if their presence is unseen or unheard. If nothing else, I just hope that this book helps reassure people that they are not alone. Even if that's just one person.

Knowing this has made such a huge difference in my life. I went through my entire childhood feeling like nobody understood me. I went through most of my adulthood feeling like something was wrong with me, wondering why I struggled so much, and why nobody liked me. For a long time, I just isolated, shut down, and carried a boat load of anger inside. If I had somebody in my life who told me these things about the Other Side and our spirit guides, I think it would have helped.

Even today, I draw so much strength from that connection to my guides and that inner knowing that I am never alone. I mean, I don't know if I would have handled my stroke the same way if I didn't know about the unconditional love and support from the Other Side. I might have gone through the whole experience a lot differently. Don't get me wrong, I would never recommend something like, "Yes, go have a stroke and you'll have a spiritual awakening and it will be great." I've been in hell these last few months and wouldn't wish this pain on anyone. But I can also appreciate the gift in it all. I've experienced so much learning and gained so much perspective.

My near-death experience solidified my belief that there is meaning in all of our lives and each of us matter so much. But you don't have to go through a stroke to gain that insight or find value in existing as a human being. Having a tough relationship, finding work-life balance, raising kids, transitioning into a different stage of life—all of these things are just as valuable as a near-death experience or spiritual awakening.

I think some people might not realize or believe that because we get mired down in the muck of being human. It can feel like you're trudging through knee-deep mud all of the time. It can make it easy to miss when you're just trying to get through the day. But you are having just as many learning opportunities as somebody like me, who is recovering from a massive stroke. So don't let anyone bring you down or tell you that you should be doing more to grow spiritually.

It's hard because humans have been conditioned to judge and put others ahead or behind themselves. It usually comes out sounding something like, "Well, yes I'm having a hard time, but oh wow, that person over there has it really bad." Or, "Man, I'm really struggling. Why is that person just succeeding without effort?" If we can get beyond that and accept that each person's life path is unique and sacred, there is no need for comparison. Each of us is doing exactly what we were meant to do, at exactly the moment we were meant to be doing it.

I can say this with confidence because when I was on the Other Side I got to cheat a little bit. I was able to see all of this and interact with my guides. I was able to view everything and everyone from a higher perspective. There, I was able to see my past, present, and future and all that it would entail, whether or not I came back. And to this day, I still get these occasional little nigglings that this is exactly where I'm supposed to be, even as far as writing this book.

Each step of the way, the perfect person has been put in my path—not only Sara who helped me write the book, but other people too. There was another person who reached out to me to help walk me through the entire process of book publishing and the steps it would take to get me out there. She helped me see what needed to happen and in what order. She also gave me a list of book editors to consider working with. As I looked through the list, the moment I saw one woman's name and looked at her website, I knew immediately that she was going to be my editor. Things like this just keep happening, and the way things have fallen into place is unreal. I am just so beyond grateful.

My hope is that each person who picks up this book finds something within it, even if it's just one thing, that helps them. Maybe a question gets answered that you have always been curious about. Maybe you get insights that can help you on your journey. Or maybe it's just an interesting, and hopefully, inspiring, story that you enjoy reading. No matter what, I hope that my intention to spread hope and light comes through.

Thank you from the bottom of my heart.

2023

Acknowledgements

Thank you, Mike, for always being there; I couldn't ask for a better dump truck. To my kids, Grace and Wyatt, for being the best and most caring kids I could ever ask for. I couldn't do any of this without you. To Michelle, for not just being my sister, but my best friend. To Cheri, I love you, thanks for always being there for me. To Megan, for matching her crazy with mine. To my parents, thank you for everything you have done. To Jenny, Darcy, Paula and Kate, thanks for sticking with me for over 30 years. To Sara Winiecki, for helping me get my thoughts on paper and making this book come to life. Lastly, to the rest of my family and friends, thank you for supporting me, not just since the stroke, but my entire life.

Made in United States
Troutdale, OR
10/24/2024

24092822R20170